FAIL YOUR WAY TO SUCCESS

To Ann,

Life will always have it's ufs and down's,
wherever there is struggle, there is
strength. Don't let Anything get in
the way of your destiny. Wishing you
every success and happiness you deserve
and more.

X

FAIL YOUR WAY TO SUCCESS

TAHAR ALI

Tahar Ali Limited

Typesetting services by BOOKOW.COM

*This book is dedicated to my children,
my sons Omar and Nihall and my daughter
Anah.
You are all my proudest achievements.*

CONTENTS

ACKNOWLEDGEMENTS

When some people are writing a book, they might think, where do I start and whom do I acknowledge? If you're looking for your book to reach thousands of readers, you need the support of an entire team to make it happen.

Firstly, I'd like to thank Lia Grace who has helped me immensely with her assistance in helping me finish this book.

I'd like to thank my sons Omar and Nihall, and my daughter Anah. My children have been my strength during the darkest days of my life, and without them, I wouldn't be here today. I'd also like to thank my mother and father who are no longer with us. I owe all that I am, or hope to be, to my parents. My sister Shameen passed away under tragic circumstances, and I thank her for all the memories.

Thank you to my best friend, Steven Summon, for staying by my side since we were four years old. Will Smith once said, *"When you hit rock bottom you'll know who your rock is when you're down there."* Steven has been my rock during the toughest days of my life, and his support, love, and inspiration has kept me focused on fulfilling my destiny.

Massive thanks to all the people who stuck by me during the tough times; my business partner Iftikhar and my sister, Shabana, whom I love dearly, with all my heart.

Finally, I am grateful to the mentors whom I have followed over the years, such as Brian Tracy, Les Brown, Jack Canfield, T. Harv Eker, Joel Osteen, James Caan, and Jane Eyre who was also my life and success coach. All these people have been instrumental in helping me through some of the worst times in my life and with their support, through their books, teachings, videos, and learning seminars, I gained the strength to write this book.

Many of the people mentioned above have dedicated much time and energy into helping me.

Finally, I would like to thank my editors Sherry Soule, Jennifer Considine, and Betty Perez for all their hard work in helping me polish my story.

Without you all, I wouldn't be able to share my message and add value to millions of people's lives.

To everyone who has purchased this book, I thank you from the bottom of my heart.

With all my love,

Tahar

PREFACE

"Who the heck is Tahar Ali, and why should I read this book?"

You'll learn more from your failures in life than you will from your successes. This book aims to teach you life lessons based on my own experiences, and to help you avoid failure and achieve success.

I hope that after you've read my book you will truly believe in yourself. I don't know what dreams you have or have been working toward, but keep in mind that "it's possible."

Most of you already know that chasing your dream is hard; it's tough changing your life. In the process of working toward your dreams, you're going to incur many disappointments, failures and a lot of pain.

To those of you who have experienced hardships: don't give up on your dreams.

The people who run toward their dreams their life will have a special kind of meaning for them.

The people who are living their dream are the ones constantly fighting to become winners and who have attached themselves to people who are living their dreams.

No matter how bad it is, or how bad it gets, say to yourself: nobody will steal my dream and "I'm going to make it."

The concepts and insights that I share with you reflect my own experiences and some of the amazing results produced by people whom I have inspired using my principles of success.

Firstly, I came from a poor background, which might be a bit of a cliché nowadays among business people, but one thing has always been rich in my life is my determination to succeed.

Personally, I have lost count of the thousands of rejections I've received and the number of times people said NO. Likewise, I've lost track of the number of people who said I could count on them but never came through.

I've had the lights and heating cut off, my car repossessed, I became homeless twice with no money to feed my children. Had numerous business failures resulting in a nervous breakdown which led to me almost committing suicide but I kept working toward my dream.

Please remember that you'll learn more from failure than you will from success.

I wasn't born successful and in a way I am glad that I wasn't because I couldn't have learned all the lessons I did in order to write this book.

If you're looking to move to a higher level of life this is something you can achieve by reading my book. By adopting the principles, I teach the results will become obvious.

I am about to share some personal stories from my life with you, some of which are really sad but I wanted to open my heart to you which few writers ever do. Making changes to your life is never easy. But I will show you how to gain self-confidence. And if I can do it, so can you.

Repeat this mantra every day: *"It's not over until I SUC-CEED."*

CHAPTER ONE

My Early Years

I was born in November 1971 in the Scottish town of Glasgow. My father was born in India in 1922 and my mother in Pakistan in 1935.

My father came to Scotland in 1958. He worked as a door-to-door salesman where he met his first wife Rosina. They married a few years later. He worked fourteen to fifteen hours a day just to earn enough to support his wife and two young girls. Times were tough back then, during the sixties era of drugs and rock and roll his wife became bored at home looking after the children.

So much so, that Rosina decided to party almost every night with her friends and visit the nightclubs; she would stroll home drunk at around four am. It wasn't long before she became an alcoholic. Literally, everything my father was earning as a wage, which was around seven pounds a week at that time was being used to fund Rosina's drinking habits.

My stepsisters suffered because my father struggled to care for them and find work to keep a roof over their heads. He was too proud to ask for help and kept brushing his problems under the carpet.

Sadly, the drinking took its toll on Rosina's health and she was diagnosed with late stage liver cancer, which was declared untreatable.

She passed away in 1968 at just forty-six, leaving behind her daughters who my father had to raise on his own. I have no idea how my father worked all the hours he did whilst looking after his children with no help at all as he didn't have any family to support him.

He managed to keep up those brutal hours for about eighteen months before it took its toll on his health and exhaustion set in. My father lived in an area of Glasgow called Crosshill where there was a large Asian presence and he was well respected in the community. It was suggested that the solution to my father's situation was to remarry through an arranged marriage, something that is common in Muslim culture today. He was against the idea of getting married again so soon after his wife's death, but by then his health had deteriorated badly and he was worried that nobody would be around to take care of his daughters.

A few months later, my father agreed to marry my mother who resided in the Pakistani village Sheikhpura. As my father couldn't travel to Pakistan for the marriage cere-mony the Nikah (Marriage) took place over the telephone. I didn't believe this at first. My initial reaction was surprise. How could anyone get married over the telephone? My mother arrived in this country in 1970.

It was difficult for my mother. She arrived in the United Kingdom to be with her husband who she had never met with just a small bag, wearing broken sandals. She didn't speak a word of English.

My father travelled to London to meet her and complete the immigration formalities so that my mother could enter the country. This was the first time she had seen my father and vice versa. Sadly, my mother took an instant dislike to him.

They barely spoke on their way back to Scotland other than my father asking her about the trip and basic formalities. The coldness of that initial meeting often made me wonder how my younger sister and I were even born.

My mother had seen photos of my stepsisters before meeting them and they all got along quite well much to my father's relief. She cared for both girls as though they were her own while my father went to work. Slowly his health started improving. He finally felt that he was getting back on track with his life and the following year I was born.

This is when my mother changed. In our Asian community it is a big deal when you give birth to a son. Even to this day in Pakistan or India people abandon baby girls in orphanages. I pray to God that every child born is healthy and that no matter what its gender, it doesn't get abandoned.

As you can imagine I was the golden child and my stepsisters no longer mattered. The level of care my stepsisters received lowered significantly. When my parents were expecting their second child, the two-bedroom apartment we lived in became too cramped for everyone to live in.

My stepsisters who were seven and eight at the time didn't really know any better. They went to school each day and loved listening to Elvis Presley.

In November of 1972 my younger sister Shabana was born. My mother was displeased that it was a girl.

My father was working longer hours because he had six people to provide for in a two-bedroom apartment and life was a real struggle.

My mother was still not pleased that my stepsisters were living at home. Finally she told my father that my stepsisters should be placed into care, a proposition that my father directly refused.

My father was a man who wanted a peaceful life and sadly his relationship with my mother deteriorated so badly that they didn't even speak to one another.

I remember my childhood from the age of five or six years old; my parents barely communicated. My father slept in the kitchen; my mother, my younger sister and I slept in one bedroom while my stepsisters slept in the other.

I never once questioned my parents about why they didn't speak during my early childhood. I was too busy playing with my friends to worry about what was going on at home. My stepsisters were good to my younger sister and me. They looked after us as if we were their own despite the way my mother treated them, which said a lot about their characters.

In life, one of the hardest things I've learned to do is to forgive. People carry anger around with them for years and blame others for their problems. Anger is just one letter away from danger. Anger is a negative emotion, which can kill your desire for success. Not only that, but anger blocks the conscious part of your brain from thinking positively and clearly.

Things in my home were quite tense. With so many people living under the same roof friction was inevitable, so my stepsisters asked my father if they could go into a care home. Having to part with his daughters at such a young age broke his heart.

My stepsisters would come to visit my sister and me whenever my mother wasn't home. I remember my father making us all dinner and telling us stories about the daft things I used to do as a baby.

He said I was a stubborn child when I was learning to walk; I kept falling down, but I always kept getting back up no matter how many times I fell. I thought nothing of it until later when I realised that this was an early indication of my determined nature.

Things were difficult for us financially. We would have to buy second-hand clothes, or rely on other people for hand-me-down garments.

My mother started working to earn some extra income; she worked long hours as a machinist in a smoky factory in Glasgow.

My father was always out at work as well; it was difficult to learn anything from my parents as I rarely saw them. When I came home from school I changed out of my school clothes and went to play with my friends. Remembering some of the mischief I got into still makes me cringe; I have the injuries and scars as constant reminders. I was a big risk-taker: I would jump from two-story buildings without hesitating, and climb over fences adorned with large "danger" signs, just for the rush. I fell a few times and once when I was eight years old a steel pipe ripped through my knee. The next day despite being barely able to walk because of the injury, I went straight back to my dangerous behaviour.

I was fearless, an essential quality for successful people. If you constantly worry about the outcome of a decision then you will never succeed. Taking risks was an everyday occurrence for me as a child and still is to this day; even though today they are a little more calculated.

I was growing up too fast, but I was also learning fast; I was a street-smart kid who wasn't afraid of anything.

Despite the fact that both of my parents worked, we were poor. Whenever I asked my father for something, his response was: "I can't afford it." I never asked my mother because I knew she sent all of her wages home to Pakistan to help provide for her own mother. If my mother ever had money left over she would put it into savings.

I remember asking for a tennis racket set because Wimbledon was on TV; I loved tennis and dreamed of winning every tournament. My father refused even though it was only ninety-nine pence. His reply was: when you earn a living you can buy your own things. As it was a passion of mine to play tennis, my determination eventually paid off and he bought me the racket. I could have just accepted NO for an answer and never have asked again!

Even when my father did say no, I did not become despondent at the rejection. I just let my determination and passion for my dream shine through instead.

You will face many rejections and feel like giving up. Make those rejections your friend and you'll be amazed at what you can achieve.

I was now ten years old, I began to understand that my parents were unhappy in their marriage. Due to the culture I was brought up in divorce was not an option. When I noticed that my mother never cooked for my father, never cared for him or loved him, I became upset. Watching my father make his own meals and eat on his own after fourteen to fifteen hours at work was quite distressing.

I recall a time when my father became quite ill and ended up in hospital. My mother didn't visit him once and when he came home she didn't even ask how he was. I was determined that if I were to ever marry, my relationship would not be like that.

It was quite heart breaking. There were so many occasions where I would see my father eating by himself so I would go over and steal some of his dinner just as an excuse to join him so that he wouldn't feel lonely.

It was quite the wakeup call for me; at ten-years-old, I was finally beginning to realise that there was no love in our home. To this day I can't recall either of my parents ever telling me that they loved me or that they were proud of me. I just thought it was normal because we lived in an Asian community where showing affection or love in front of others is taboo.

My home life became tougher when my stepsister Shameen, became addicted to glue sniffing.

Although my father was tired of Shameen's erratic behaviour, he stood by her and supported her without judgment. Even if she were found in the street at four am he would bring her home, put her head in cold water until she came around, and then make her dinner. This was the first time I saw how big-hearted my father actually was. He forgave very easily and never held a grudge.

CHAPTER TWO

Time Away from Home

I needed some time away from home. Luckily I had my first school field trip; I was excited as it was the first time I would be away from home for five days.

On the field trip, I felt independent like a grown man who was finally realising that he was destined to become something.

In the evenings a group of us boys went to areas of the estate that were out of bounds. If our escapades involved anything risky, I was the first to try it. I didn't care about the consequences, as just having the freedom to do what I wanted meant more to me than getting into trouble would have if I'd have been caught.

I had the most amazing time of my life; I made new friends and some of the girls even developed crushes on me because of my risk-taking nature.

I was on top of the world and couldn't wait to get back home to tell my parents about it. Sadly for me I would have to tell my story twice as my parents were never in the same room as one another.

However, when I returned home my mother was quite ill. She was struggling to get out of bed. I asked her what was wrong and she told me that she was okay, she just had a bad fever…but there was blood on the sheets. I had never seen anything like this before and I knew it was serious. I told my father who called for the doctor. The doctor said my mother would need to go to hospital straight away because she was bleeding internally. She was rushed into surgery for an operation on her bowel.

She had to have a blood transfusion and was in such a bad way. For the first time in my life I prayed and begged God to make her better. I made a promise to God that I would stop getting into trouble as long as he didn't take her away from me. I didn't know whether God was listening but even at such a young age I had faith, a consequence of all the years spent at the mosque after school.

My mother was in hospital for almost three weeks and I went to visit her every day. During this time I kept my promise to God, which was an achievement in itself.

Finally she came home and her friends came to visit her to see how she was. I could tell she was tired; it felt as though she had aged overnight from all the stress of being ill.

My mother was incredibly resilient. She wasn't a quitter, and was determined to get back to work. Almost four weeks had passed since she was able to work and she was worried about her mother in Pakistan whether she would be coping without her financial support.

Around six weeks later she made a full recovery and re-turned to work.

CHAPTER THREE

First Job

When I was twelve years old things were getting tough at home financially so I told my father that I wanted to get a job. He told me that I was too young and that no one would give me a job. However, seeing as I never took NO for an answer I went straight out and met one of my father's friends Munir who had a market stall selling denim clothing. I asked if he could give me a job helping at his stall but he also said that I was too young. Again I refused to take NO for an answer. I persuaded him by offering to work for free; if I was rubbish then he could just fire me. He had nothing to lose.

Munir was amazed at my determination and agreed that I could work on Saturdays and Sundays from eight am to four-thirty pm. I was told not to be late. Something I have learned over the years is to always be on time. I am a stickler for punctuality because I respect others people's time as well as my own. On my first day working for Munir, I unloaded the stock from the van and carried it to the stall so that it could be set up in time for opening. I worked hard; my arms ached from all the lifting but I had something to prove.

The stall got busy around lunchtime. My job was to act as a deterrent to potential thieves who would try to steal things by distracting the owner. This was not something I was used to as the only experience I had with shoplifters was my stepsister Shameen.

Once the lunchtime rush settled down, I was given £1 ($2) to buy lunch. I thought 'wow!' The most I'd ever possessed was fifty pence so already I had doubled my money.

When I went to buy my lunch, I noted what the other market stalls were selling and how busy they were. I wished that I could get my own business one day and make money. However my dreams were perturbed by the fact that I only had £1 to my name. I told myself to stop dreaming so big, get some lunch and get my ass back to work before I was late.

I finished my first day at the stall and loaded the stock back into the van before getting a lift home. Munir asked me if I'd enjoyed my first day and if I was coming back tomorrow. I said yes and that I'd loved it. I got such a high from the hustle and bustle of the market. There was no way I was going to tell Munir that my arms hurt and that I was exhausted. The next day I was on time and ready to work.

During my lunch break that day I went to buy chips. This time I paid more attention to some of the methods people were using to peddle their items. I watched as crowds gathered around certain stalls to see what the buzz was about; I deduced that the popularity of the stall depended mainly on the salesperson's character. I thought 'wow!', and it seemed that everyone else did also as they started to pull their money out buying these items. It wasn't the actual product that affected the sale; it was the techniques used by the salesperson. Their selling techniques were such that they had people literally queuing up to pay them, something I had never before.

If you've ever had a sales job, you will know that a sales job is often a default because there are no other jobs available.

No matter what it is that you do, whether you are a dentist, a solicitor, or an accountant; you're a salesperson. After all, you need to be able to sell your service in order to attract customers. It is similar to how you behave on a job interview; you have to market yourself effectively in order to be accepted by your prospective employer.

I knew that if I studied the way the successful salespeople marketed their items, it wouldn't be long before I could open my own business.

After my third week working for Munir he gave me £10 ($15). I asked, "What was this for?"

He said that it was my salary for the days I'd worked. I was completely shocked; I didn't know what to say. Even the words "Thank You" took a while to come out of my mouth. £10! It was more money than I'd ever had before and the satisfaction I felt because I'd earned it was sensational.

I couldn't wait to get home to tell my father, I would never need to ask him for money again because I was earning my own wages. My first instinct was to spend the money on things I'd been wanting for months like toys and games. However, as I knew money was tight at home I gave the ten pounds to my father and asked him to keep it to help with the bills.

He refused to take my money, so I asked him if he would keep it safe to prevent me from spending it.

Weeks went by. I continued working at the market stall and loved every minute. As a risk-taker I was a quick learner. One of the skills I developed from watching the market traders at work was the ability to listen to and understand five different conversations at once. We all have skills, we all learn. After all we are born into this world naked and speechless; our peers teach us everything we know.

Keep in mind, as a child you're only born with two fears; the fear of loud noises and the fear of falling. Every other fear is learned; something you'll read about later on in my book.

At this point, things were going great. I was earning money and giving it to my father to save so that someday I could start my own business.

CHAPTER FOUR

A Business Initiative

In 1983, computers were becoming popular. I recall that the ZX Spectrum was released onto the market the year before and everyone seemed to be anticipating the Commodore 64. This was the opportunity that I'd been waiting for; I could see a gap in the market. People wanted to buy computer games but not at the extortionate retail prices.

I thought: what about selling second-hand games? Once a kid finishes a game, or becomes bored with it, they then want to move on to another. I asked Munir if I could use a section of his stall to sell games. At first, he thought I was crazy. Who was going to buy used games from a market stall?

But I was determined. I asked him to let me trial the venture for a few weeks. If it didn't work out I would give him back my wages. I visited all of my friends asking them for their old games; I told them that I planned to sell the games and make some extra cash so they could buy new ones. If I didn't manage to sell their games, I would return them.

I sold the proposition to them using the same techniques I'd learned whilst observing the market traders. I told my friends that if I sold their games, I would split the earnings with them so they had nothing to lose. I would do all the sales work. This method allowed me to build up an initial stock of fifty different games without having to invest any money. The way I saw it, I was making fifty percent of something as opposed to one-hundred percent of nothing.

Many people who require funding for their businesses are reluctant to give up an equity share. They can't see the value someone might bring to them. It's not difficult to understand that hiring someone who can take your company to a million pound profit and getting 50% of that money, is more beneficial than earning only one-hundred thousand pounds on your own, and getting 100%.

On my first day selling games, I decided to drum up some customers. I visited the other stalls where I knew other young people who were helping their parents. I told them that I had some of the latest games for sale at less than half of the retail price. As you can imagine, everyone became inquisitive when they realised they were getting a bargain and all the kids gathered round my stall, much to the amusement of our family friend.

Before long kids were running back to their parents to get money; that day I sold ten games at the value of £50 ($75). This wasn't bad for a kid who earned ten pounds a weekend! I had started my own business and in one day more than doubled my money. When I gave my friends their share, word spread and many more games came my way. Kids wanted the extra cash to buy new games, while people with less money wanted to save by purchasing my used games. It was a win-win situation.

In no time at all, I had amassed a fair bit of cash. However, I slipped up in not paying attention to others. I never thought for a second that someone might copy my idea.

Before I knew it, there were almost twenty different stalls selling games and business was slowing down. I became quite disheartened. I hadn't realized that while I was watching the other sellers on my lunch break; they were doing the same thing. I became complacent.

Never get complacent!

It wasn't long before other stalls starting selling new games at half the retail price. I wondered how they could manage this not realising that the games were counterfeit copies. This was not something I wanted to do.

My mother became ill again and I had to give up my job to look after her. We went back to the doctors and soon it became clear that my mother had blood in her stools. I didn't know how to process this information; I just pleaded with the doctor to make my mother better as I hated seeing her sick.

My mother and father never spoke, so it was out of character for her to share anything with him. Each time we visited the doctors, she told me not to say anything to him.

CHAPTER FIVE

Learning to Forgive

Eventually, my mother was sent to see a specialist who referred her to see another one. I struggled to keep up with the amount of hospital and doctor appointments whilst attending school and staying on top of my homework.

Things were stressing me out; I missed playing with my friends and I was falling behind at school, sometimes even falling asleep in class. I was so behind with my work that I was placed in the bottom half of the class.

In January 1986, I thought that this year would have to be better than the last few. My mother was still seriously ill. I remember exactly on the 14th of January whilst on a visit with her to hospital, the doctors asked for my father because they had something important to discuss. They admitted my mother and when I got home I told my father everything. He went to the hospital straight away and met the doctors, who informed him that my mother had bowel cancer and about six months left to live.

At first I was shocked as I didn't know what to do and I felt sick. I was closer to my mother than my father. I kept saying to God: I haven't gotten into any trouble; I've worked hard and behaved. Is this what I get in return for my faith in you? I was looking for someone to blame. I didn't know if I was more angry or upset. I never thought about what my father must have been going through; this was the second time he had to stand by as his wife was diagnosed with terminal cancer.

Things changed at home; my father stayed home to look after the children. He was a man who more or less wanted a quiet life. Some people would call that a life, but I call it a waste.

Why?

Firstly, you were chosen from four-hundred million sperm for a reason. You have a purpose. No manufacturer makes a product without knowing its purpose; you as an individual are no different.

I visited my mother in hospital every day. My father came as well and I saw a side to him that I had never seen before; it could only be called love. He looked after my mother, helped her in and out of bed, took her to the bathroom, gave her water and food to eat and made her as comfortable as he possibly could. I couldn't believe what I was seeing; my mother never spoke to this man. She never cooked for him or cleaned for him and when he was ill in hospital, she never went to see him. My mother never publicly acknowledged that my father was her husband, yet here he was doing all of the things my mother had never done for him.

I asked my father why, and I will never forget what he said.

"Tahar, when someone has wronged you, learn to forgive. With that forgiveness, God gives you the strength to

move forward. If you hold a grudge, you achieve nothing but bitterness, sorrowfulness and regret. Don't ever live a life of regret my son. Only regret what you haven't done."

Forgiving people who have wronged you is hard. I know that only too well. My lesson in forgiveness came early at just fourteen years old.

Some people hold grudges for years and end up becoming bitter, when they could have just forgiven the person who wronged them and moved on with their life.

CHAPTER SIX

Tough Times

Toward the end of March 1986, my mother lost so much weight that she had to be fed through a tube; I could barely recognise her.

On one visit whilst I was sat at her bedside holding her hand, she looked at me for some time. I knew what she was thinking: that she wouldn't ever see her children again.

My father came back into the room with a jug of fresh cold water, she turned to him and said: "Please forgive me for what I have done to you." as the tears ran down her face. He simply replied, "Don't be silly. There is nothing to forgive."

She asked if he would look after the children once she had gone. His reply was, "You're not going anywhere, woman." He laughed off the remark but he was crying. He did his best to hide the tears so that my mother couldn't see them.

Ten days later, we got a call from the hospital saying that my mother was in a lot of pain and was asking for her family. We went to the hospital to see her; she was very distressed. The doctors had given her so much morphine that she could barely speak. Her cheeks were pale and yellow. I couldn't bear to see her like that so I asked my father if I could go home.

He took us home but went straight back to the hospital to look after her. He returned home at around one am and told us that mum had gone to Heaven.

I felt numb and sick but for some reason I couldn't cry. My first thought was that my mother was no longer suffering or in pain. I was relieved. I asked my father if we could go to hospital to say goodbye.

When we arrived, my mother was in the same room; it was as though she were asleep. I thought the doctors were just confused. I held her hand, hoping she would wake up because her son was at her bedside. I stroked her arm, saying, "I am here, please wake up, please wake up."

That was when I cried. I became so hysterical that I had to be taken out of the room until I calmed down and came back to my senses.

I didn't want my mother to go away. Sometimes life is tough and my life was about to get much tougher.

In the Muslim tradition a funeral must be carried out as soon as possible. My mother was blessed to have her funeral on a Friday with a turnout of over one thousand people. Both of my parents were well known in our community. When I saw my mother in the coffin I broke down. I knew I had to be strong until after the funeral.

When I arrived at the graveyard I saw the six-foot hole dug into the ground where my mother was to be buried. I held her coffin and helped place it into the grave. It finally sunk in; there was no way I could ever see my mother again.

CHAPTER SEVEN

Breaking Out the Comfort Zone

After my mother passed away, many people in the local community stopped by our home to pay their respects. I just wanted to be left alone to grieve in peace.

When I went back to high school my friends proved to be a distraction from my problems. Being close to them could transform my sad mood into a happy one.

I love to smile. Over the years even during my darkest days, I have learned that the ability to smile can make a huge difference to your day. It can even affect the way people react to you and your general wellbeing can improve dramatically. If I ever feel down I think of this quote: "A smile is a curve that straightens everything." After all, it only takes thirteen muscles to smile and around one hundred and twelve muscles to frown.

My schoolteachers treated me differently; they were overly nice to me. I was used to getting a rollicking for not doing my homework or for not paying attention in class. At the time I couldn't see the point in getting an education.

I felt dejected; I just wanted to be sixteen years old so that I could leave school legally and get a job. My view was who needs an education to make money, as long as you're smart and intelligent? School had become a chore; I was missing classes and mixing with the wrong crowd. I would spend my time joining gangs and getting into fights just for fun. I stole cars and learned to drive at fifteen. I loved the adrenaline rush and it felt as though I was living life on the edge. I was becoming distanced from my family and became stubborn, selfish, and arrogant.

This was a brand new side of my personality. I usually had a nice disposition. I loved to help other people and treated everyone with the utmost respect. This was the way my mother and father had taught me to be.

The change in my personality was borderline dangerous but I was too far gone to care. At school, I got into trouble with my teachers and came close to getting expelled. However, they knew my behaviour wasn't representative of my true character; it was just a phase I was going through following the death of my mother.

My new friendship group kept telling me that the education system was failing everyone so why bother getting one. Many people still believe this and some of them may be right.

Most students who've just graduated from university are in debt. They have to get a job quickly to clear their student loans whilst trying to keep a roof over their heads. They spend years studying only to end up working as a waiter or flipping burgers. They do not get to use their PhD.

People ask me the question: Should I continue with my education? My response is yes, but I tell them to run an online business to earn extra money while they study so that they don't end up in debt.

Most people don't want to do that so they find an excuse not to.

My father was looking after me full time and I could tell the trouble I was getting into was taking its toll on him. He still had to contend with my stepsister Shameen and her drug addiction. He had started to drive me to and from school just to make sure I attended.

CHAPTER EIGHT

Dating in Secret

I was fifteen years old so only had to endure one more year of school; it would pass quickly.

My life changed when I started to fancy a girl. Her name was Angela McGregor; she was from a white background and thought I was the Karate Kid, Ralph Macchio.

As I am from an Asian background, dating a non-Asian girl was just asking for trouble in our community. My father was very well respected; people would tell me that I was bringing such shame to my family by dating someone outside our culture.

We dated in secret. We'd go to the cinema together or out for a bite to eat. However, the whole school knew that we were dating and it didn't take long for word to get back to my father.

That night I went home and my father said he wanted to talk to me. I knew I hadn't been in trouble lately so I couldn't think what it might be.

He said, "I hear you're dating a non-Asian girl at school." My first instinct was to deny it but I couldn't lie to my father. After all this man had looked after me, driven me to school and back and provided for me after my mother had passed away, so it would have been incredibly disrespectful to lie. I came clean and told him that yes I was. I didn't know what the problem was but I was told that the relationship must end. I was quite gutted as I really liked Angela but some things are just not meant to be.

My father had plenty of people to advise him but many of these people had problems in their own homes. Sharing advice is very common in the Asian community even to this day.

What I didn't realise was that members of our community were telling my father to take me to Pakistan and sort out an arranged marriage. They thought he should get me settled down before I went off the rails.

What the hell? This reaction was spurned purely by the fact that I was dating a non-Asian girl at school.

My father decided to follow their advice and behind my back sought out a girl in Pakistan for me to marry.

CHAPTER NINE

Employers and Exploitation

At sixteen, I left school. I was spending time with people who were a bad influence; we would steal cars at night. I needed to start earning a living and quickly found work at a Cash and Carry stacking shelves and creating displays. I was hired in the toy section, which suited me because I got to play with all the latest toys. It was hard work; I began at nine am and often came home at ten pm with only one day off during the week. This limited the amount of time I could spend with the wrong friends so in a way it was a blessing as it meant I couldn't get into much trouble. I used to walk to work as the Cash and Carry was only two miles away from my home.

My employers were like slave drivers. They rarely gave me a break and never let me sit down to rest. No matter how hard I worked for them, I never seemed to work hard enough. If something had been done incorrectly, they would publically humiliate their employees. I'd been brought up to look out for others so I would always defend my fellow employees. This earned me a harsh scolding and I would be humiliated for speaking out on their behalf.

I didn't care about getting fired because I knew I would find something else. Most people put up with poor treatment in the workplace because they're scared of losing their job. They worry about how they will pay their bills and mortgage and put food on the table. When an employer knows this, they can take advantage and mistreat you further as they know you won't quit because you're in desperate need of the money.

If you are unhappy in your job or for the company your work for then get creative, come up with some ideas about what you're going to do with your life and write them down to pursue them. You shouldn't sell yourself short of your worth. I did so in this job working for just £65 ($95) a week.

Just £65 a week, to be humiliated, treated like dirt and worked like a slave. But I didn't want to quit because I wasn't a quitter. I wanted to save money and make my father proud because I was making a living on my own. So I put up with the mistreatment.

I never told my father how things were in my workplace and if he ever asked me how work was, I would reply that I was doing okay and working hard. Had he known the real situation he would have been quite upset that his son wasn't happy in the workplace.

Eventually, things became so bad that I struggled to cope. I lost weight from not eating properly and didn't get the proper rest or time off that I needed. Christmas was fast approaching so the Cash and Carry was getting busier. I was packing shelves as fast as they were being emptied which to my employer looked as though I hadn't done any work. It wasn't long before I was hauled in front of the boss and given a massive scolding for slacking off. If he had checked the stock inventory, he would have seen that the stock had actually been sold, but he seemed to prefer belittling me rather than fact checking.

Always remember that if someone is belittling you, that person is being little.

On Christmas Eve, I received my salary; there was a blue envelope next to my cash. I thought nothing of the envelope because it wasn't labelled, so I binned it. Later I got a phone call from a friend at work asking how much I'd gotten as a Christmas bonus. I asked: What bonus? He said it was in the blue envelope; I'd just thought it was an envelope and binned it. Luckily, it was at the top of the garbage bin and I opened it to find £15 ($25) inside.

My first reaction was rage. I had worked twelve to thirteen hour days for three months standing on my feet all day with no breaks. I'd suffered the boss's humiliation for just £15. Maybe I should have been grateful; not many sixteen year olds got that kind of money during that era but it wasn't just about the money. I was already selling myself short of my worth for £65 a week, so to receive £15 for three months' work equated to fifteen pence a day.

This was the last straw. I snapped and as soon as I returned to work after Boxing Day, I marched into my boss's office with the blue envelope and the £15. I told him to shove the £15 and the blue envelope up his ass!

I gave him quite a tirade of abuse before telling him that I wouldn't be coming back to work and that one day Karma would bring him bad fortune because of the way he treated people.

I realized that I had behaved in the same way as my boss because of how I had been treated. It was only natural for me to end up that way. Lots of employers treat their staff badly, only for the same staff to become employers themselves and replicate this treatment. After all, behaviour breeds behaviour.

You cannot have poor behaviour standards in business. It doesn't matter how hard the work is, how much pressure you're under, or how much you're struggling. If you vent your frustration and anger at your employees, they won't give you 100%.

I have been an employer many times myself and I was nice to my employees beyond their expectations, so much so that they took advantage of my kindness. Finding a balance is important in business but it's not always easy to achieve. Being a leader is never easy.

If your actions inspire others to dream more, learn more, do more, and become more than they already are, then you'll become a leader.

Sometimes people will hear you better if you speak with a voice of compassion rather than one of authority. People want to be understood, not lectured.

I quickly found another job working as a shop assistant in a video store renting the latest releases. I loved my new job; I was able to see all the latest movies for free. I only worked five days a week, from ten am to seven pm and I was getting paid £120 ($180) per-week, which was almost double my salary at the Cash and Carry. With this new company, I even got a lunch break and I could sit down if there were no customers in the store. However, even though I loved my job my area manager, a woman called Kathleen was very difficult to work with. The other staff had warned me about her and true enough she was an atrocious human being. So far, my experience working for bosses and managers wasn't great.

Honestly, I didn't know what this woman's problem was and I didn't care about her problem, either. I just wanted to do my job to the best of my ability and I did not want to get mistreated by my boss. But Kathleen's authority had gone to her head. She didn't just have a chip on her shoulder— she had a brick on it.

My father seemed happy for me; as far as he was concerned, I had a decent job.

CHAPTER TEN

Arranged Marriage

I'd just had my seventeenth birthday and my father told me that I should ask for time off from work to go on holiday to Pakistan.

I never thought anything of it. I asked my dad why we were going to Pakistan; he replied that we were going to visit family and take a break.

I was excited about flying on a Boeing 747. I was quite the plane enthusiast and had dreamed of being a pilot as a child so that I could fly my mother around the world. That dream died after she passed away but I still had an infatuation with planes.

Relatives met us at Pakistan Airport, most of whom I'd never met.

We had planned to stay with a relative for the duration of our holiday.

After a few days, my jet lag wore off and I settled in quite nicely. I made new friends and met my family. It wasn't long before I decided to get into some mischief. My father had warned me to stay out of trouble because things were different in Pakistan. We needed to show respect because we were guests here. This piece of advice went in one ear and out the other.

I loved to break the rules, the more rules I broke, the bigger the adrenaline rush. If someone told me I couldn't do something, I would tell them to watch me.

I now set my own rules, based on some key principles, which work much better for me.

Think back to the best meal you've ever had. It didn't taste amazing by chance. Whoever made it for you will have followed a recipe. The first time they attempted it, they probably made a few mistakes, likewise with the second time, but by the sixth attempt, they probably would have mastered the recipe.

The same principle applies with success-don't quit! You may have struggled to ride a bicycle or drive a car, but with practise, you mastered it. Every skill is learnable and every bad habit is un-learnable.

One day in Pakistan, I spent my time learning how to fly a kite. It was great fun but when it started to get dark, I decided to go home so that my father wouldn't worry about me. When I arrived I overheard him speaking to a few of the elders and realised they were discussing an arranged marriage for me.

What bloody marriage? I was only seventeen and way too young to get married. Before I left Scotland, my friends had teased me that kids who go off the rails are taken to Pakistan to get married. I told them that would never happen to me as we were only going on holiday.

But there was nothing further from the truth. I had been conned; the holiday was pretence and I was actually here to get married.

After the elders left, I spoke to my father. He told me that they had been discussing my future bride. At first, I was relieved as it sounded like the marriage would happen in the far-distant future. That's when he dropped the bombshell; a bride had been chosen for me. It was a girl called Fozia. I knew Fozia and I told my father that she wasn't my type; she still sucked her thumb at sixteen! But he informed me that he had already agreed and given his word.

As the shock sank in, even I the person who never took NO for an answer couldn't utter the word NO to this. After a few minutes I told him that there was no way I was going to marry that girl and he couldn't force me to. My father was a well-respected man and his word was his bond. Now he had to break all of his principles just to keep his son happy. I explained that this was my life he was talking about; my future and it would be ruined if I couldn't choose who I spent my life with.

Sadly I had to play on his emotions. I was his only son, did he hate me so much that he wanted to ruin my life.

I was shocked when he replied that whatever made me happy, made him happy. I couldn't believe what I was hearing that he would agree to something I asked for; it was like getting blood from a stone. He said he would speak to the girl's family and explain that his son wasn't agreeable to the marriage. My relief was immense but I felt sorry for my father who had to break the news to this girl's family as they had made all of the arrangements for our marriage.

Sometimes, you need to remember that your destiny is already written; even the person you're meant to be with is fated. There is a set time and place for you to meet them.

Being single doesn't mean you're lonely, it just means that the right person hasn't entered your life yet.

He took a fair bit of abuse for going back on his word. However, he stuck to his guns for the sake of my happiness. I had never seen a determined side to his personality; it was always my mother who showed determination and ambition so this was a new experience for me. He made it clear that he would not control his son's future and if anyone had an issue with this then he didn't care whether they liked him or not.

I recall one of his quotes: "Don't worry if anyone doesn't like you, as long as you like you, that is all that matters and what gets you through it."

He was a wise man although I ignored most of his advice. I thought I knew better back then but somehow I remember all of his sayings, advice and quotes today.

I was counting down the days until we were due to travel home. It was then that I first saw Nazia, a girl I took a fancy to. She seemed lovely and my father caught me looking and asked me if I liked her. I told him that I did and he asked if I wanted him to discuss a marriage proposal with her parents. I said that I would rather wait a few years until I was ready but I would be happy for him to make an engagement proposal with her parents. He was quite happy with that but sadly Nazia's parents weren't. They asked for the concrete bond of Nikah (Marriage without consummation) only, since they knew my father had gone back on his word regarding the first marriage he'd lined up for me.

Nazia's parents didn't want to arrange an engagement that went on for years only to realise that their daughter was no longer of any age to marry. This is common in the Pakistani community. Girls are married young because their parents believe that once they turn twenty-five, no one will want to marry them. However I didn't want my father having to lose face again so I agreed.

Before I knew it, I was a married man! I had no regrets and a few days later I returned to Scotland while Nazia remained in Pakistan.

While I was on the flight back home, I thought about my parents; they'd had an arranged marriage and would my life end up like theirs?

These negative thoughts were going through my head because I knew how unhappy my parents had been and I didn't want the same situation for myself. However the positive side of my brain was telling me not to worry. I knew what they had been through so I just needed to work hard to ensure that I didn't suffer the same fate.

CHAPTER ELEVEN

Returning Home

When we arrived in Scotland it was snowing and cold which was a far cry from the sunshine and warm climate of Pakistan.

I had a few days to rest before I had to return to work. When I returned Kathleen decided to change my job role. Instead of working permanently in the local branch, which was two hundred yards from my home, I was to work in any branch that needed cover. This was difficult as I didn't know where I would be from one day to the next.

Six months had passed since Nazia and I got married. I was writing to Nazia or occasionally speaking over the phone so I was building up a rapport with her. Consequently, I didn't mind getting sent to different branches by Kathleen at first. However, it could take me up to two hours to travel to and from work. I was never reimbursed for my travel time or expenses so once again I was feeling dejected.

Because I was married my goal was to save enough money to buy my first home. I already had the money that my father had kept for me, so I knew it wouldn't be long before

I had a decent amount of cash to put toward a mortgage. However, that dream seemed very far away. I was getting sick of my job but I needed to be in employment so that Nazia's visa application would be approved allowing her to enter the country. I had to stick it out.

I decided that the minute the Nazia's approval came through I would quit my job. This time I was smart because I already had a job lined up with a competitor who had interviewed me the month before. A few months later Nazia's visa came through and I left my job at the video shop.

The transition between jobs was straightforward because I knew the system and the business inside out and didn't need training. I worked hard and I do so to this day. I am often asked how I manage to balance my work life and my personal life.

My answer is consistent: I don't. Even when I am on holiday, I work a few hours at least; likewise at the weekend. My philosophy is work hard whilst working. Many people would disagree with this theory but take into consideration that those who are at the top of the mountain didn't just fall there; they worked and worked to get there.

If you want to be successful, you need to do more than what is required of you. If someone is struggling with their workload help them out rather than watch them suffer and struggle. You may not like this person but someone will notice how hard you're working.

Some people say success or promotion is all about luck.

I learned that the harder you work, the luckier you get, so work hard and keep doing so; you'll see the results.

CHAPTER TWELVE

Striving for Independence

Nazia arrived in Scotland in March of 1990. I went to pick her up from London; similarly to the way my father collected my mother when she arrived into the country. Nazia however did like me and we had a pleasant enough conversation.

Nazia was a quiet woman; she didn't say much. She was soft spoken and humble. I liked that about her but none of my sisters did at the time.

I was working long hours and Nazia was pregnant with our first child. I was thrilled at the thought of being a father but I was also scared because I was so young. It was difficult for Nazia as she was at home all day. She became bored with no one to speak to; my arrival home from work was the highlight of her day. I would see her waiting at the window in the same place I used to sit and wait for my mother. I really felt for Nazia because I knew how difficult it was for her being away from her entire family and all of her friends, living in a completely different country and not being able to speak English.

I was saving a large chunk of my salary because I wanted my own home. It was a dream of mine to be independent.

I saved every penny I could and if I had any additional money, I put it toward buying baby clothes and any other items we would need for our newborn. Things at home were tough because my sisters weren't getting along with Nazia and my father didn't do a thing to help the situation. He had retired so he just wanted to enjoy his pension; he spent his free time meeting up with his friends for tea and biscuits.

I needed around £1200 ($1800) for the deposit and with a baby on the way I decided to take a second job. I got a job with my stepsister Parveen's husband who worked as a chef. At first I thought that I wouldn't enjoy this new job because I was only there for the money. However, I loved it and my stepsister's husband taught me how to cook. In no time at all I was covering for him while he completed other tasks. The downside of having a second job was having to work such long hours; I wasn't getting home until almost one am. It didn't bother me because I was young and full of energy and enthusiasm, so it was quite easy to manage.

Most people get fed up with life at the age of twenty-five, until they get buried at sixty-five; they complain that they have no energy. Once you let that thought process into your mind, it's hard to change your attitude. When you have days where your mind tells you that you can't do something or days when you want to give up, dig deep and remember what you're doing it all for; that's what will get you through.

After a few months of working seven days a week I had raised the money I needed. I just needed to find a home to buy. After work Nazia and I spent hours visiting estate agents, touring the neighbourhoods to find our first home. It wasn't easy; we must have viewed forty to fifty houses. Eventually we viewed a property that had just come onto the market. I placed an offer with my solicitor the next morning.

I went to see a mortgage broker the following day; I thought I had enough money saved for a deposit. I hadn't take into account the fees and insurance costs that would be incurred with the loan. This caused a problem since the only option left was to buy a one-hundred percent mortgage, which meant that I had no equity in the property. I asked my broker to get me the best deal available, which he did and although the cost was higher than what I had budgeted for, it was affordable because I was earning a good income with my current job.

It took eight weeks to complete the sale but my father didn't know that I had just bought a house and was preparing to move out.

CHAPTER THIRTEEN

A New Arrival

In January 1991, Nazia was past her due date so the doctors induced labour. I was in the theatre whilst Nazia was giving birth. We named the child Omar and he was a healthy boy for which I was extremely grateful to God.

After Nazia gave birth, she became severely ill because she had caught an infection while in the hospital. We were told it was German measles; my wife had to be kept isolated on a separate ward, which was difficult for her because mothers need early bonding time with their child after birth. I really felt sorry for her.

When we arrived back at my father's house everyone was obsessed with my son, especially my father. I actually think he spent more time looking after my boy than I did. Nazia and I didn't have much for our son but we had a crib. As Nazia had just recovered from German measles she couldn't breast-feed so we had to feed him powdered bottled milk.

About four weeks later Nazia suggested that we tell my father about the new house. I told her that it was going to be difficult because we didn't have any furniture or anything else we needed for our new home.

Telling my father was difficult. He had grown attached to my son, and would have to part with both his son and his grandson now. I kept putting it off; I couldn't find the courage to tell him.

Another week or so passed, and I finally plucked up the courage to tell him I was leaving home. The look on his face said it all; it was a look of utter devastation and I felt like total crap.

He wasn't angry but puzzled. He said that I had everything I needed here so why would I buy a house? I explained that I wanted to be my own man and look after my family.

To my shock, he told me that I could leave as I'd never make it on my own. I reminded him that I didn't have anything for my home yet; I couldn't just leave as we had nowhere to sleep. He told me that it wasn't his problem and that I should go and be my own man and figure it out.

We all face tough decisions sometimes. Most of us worry so much about them, fear kicks in, which then stops us from taking a step forward.

I was never afraid but the thought of moving out of my comfort zone scared me. So many doubts were going through my head. I didn't know if I would cope sleeping on the floor, having no money without my father's support.

I doubted my ability to make it simply because I lived with my parents. However, throughout my entire life I had been a massive risk-taker so I told my father I would leave that night.

I had to make a few journeys back and forth to transfer all of our clothes and baby stuff to the new house.

I could tell by my father's eyes that he was quite distraught; I had completely broken his heart. I was in tears as well. He asked me if he could say goodbye to his grandson and cuddled him for a long time. He hugged Nazia but not me. I had finally left the home I grew up in and I did so crying.

CHAPTER FOURTEEN

Going it Alone

That first night in our new home the whole house was bare. We had no furniture, nothing besides our clothes and the baby crib.

It sunk in that I had left my comfort zone when I realised we had no blankets. Nazia and I slept on the rock hard floor, which was icy cold. I felt bad about leaving my father; it was cutting me up more than I thought it would.

I eventually turned on the heating and fell asleep for a few hours before waking up to my son crying.

After he was fed I needed a glass of water; I felt dehydrated from what seemed like the longest night of my life. I realised I didn't even have a glass to drink from; I had to place my mouth next to the tap.

My stressed mind was already telling me that I should have stayed with my father.

One thing I learned from this experience is that you can't have a better tomorrow if you're thinking about yesterday. If you listen to your fears, you will never know how great a person you could become.

I could have given into my doubts and fears but I had a point to prove. I had to prove to my father that I could be independent and if I didn't do something fast; his parting words to me would become embedded in my subconscious.

I decided to keep on at my second job so I could earn some extra money to buy furniture and basic essentials like cutlery, plates and cups for my home.

I was saving money every week and purchasing everything I needed to make my house a home.

By the time I paid the mortgage, gas, electric, phone bill, bought baby milk, baby food, nappies, new clothes for my son, we had little money left for food.

The reality of being my own man finally kicked in and I realised how difficult it must have been for my parents to provide for us as a family. I worried that the rest of my life was going to be a struggle like this just about making ends meet every week.

Most people face a similar struggle. You may be doing so right now and you might be looking for ways to improve your current situation.

Don't doubt yourself by saying things would be better if only you had a better job that paid more money. Or if you could get some extra cash, that would make a difference. Ask yourself this: are you learning new skills to improve your situation or just complaining about it?

CHAPTER FIFTEEN

Financial Pressure

I was very fortunate to be in employment; however as the economy was in recession, business was slow for my employer. I was worried that it wouldn't be long before they let me go. Interest rates were rising fast. My mortgage payments had almost doubled. Even when I did manage to earn more money, it was being swallowed up by interest charges. I didn't want to go to my father for financial help; I knew he would just tell me that he'd told me so.

Nazia was pregnant with our second child and things were about to get a lot tougher. Money was scarce and with another mouth to feed, I was beginning to worry about how we would survive. I had never been a worrier but even I succumbed to this anxiety about what was going on in the economy; it began eating me up on a daily basis.

Worry is a negative emotion and shuts down your subconscious mind by confusing your brain. Worrying is like being on a treadmill; it will give you something to do but it won't get you anywhere. When you agonize over something you will become unhappy. Whatever you're worrying about may never actually happen.

Sadly I hadn't learnt these lessons back then but I can give you this advice based from my own experience. Many people will tell you that you don't need to worry; a standard reply is: "Easier said than done."

No matter how bad you think things are, someone out there is facing an even bigger struggle than you are. Try to appreciate what you do have, no matter how little that may be and you'll override the worry in your head. You should practice this habit for at least twenty-one consecutive days.

Do what you can to eliminate worry or stress. Don't believe everything the media says about the economy it will not help you. When I was struggling, interest rates were becoming beyond a joke. Businesses were going bust and unemployment was reaching an all-time high. Thousands of people's homes were being repossessed and the cost of living was rising. My employer was laying people off and at first I thought I was safe, as I'd survived the first and second rounds of cutbacks.

I was barely able to sleep at night; thoughts kept running through my head. I worried about how we would survive if I lost my job, or if I had no savings and mortgage debt.

A month later my father came to visit me unexpectedly to see how I was doing. He'd seen my house and seemed quite pleased that I had managed to buy things for my home and provide for my children but he didn't know how much I was truly struggling. At the time I would never have shared it with him as I know what his response would have been.

Nazia made my father his dinner and he ate and played with my son. He noticed that we didn't have a TV. I explained that we didn't really have time to watch TV; I didn't want to tell him that I couldn't afford one. He offered to buy us one as a house-warming gift. I told him to save his money. I was full of pride and wanted to show my father that I was managing it on my own. All I wanted to hear was that my father was really proud of me.

One thing I have learned is that no one to this day has ever choked to death by swallowing their pride!

I was falling behind with the bills and my debts for electricity and gas were rising. Before I knew it I owed around £300 ($450) in arrears.

To avoid getting disconnected I did what most people do, which is to use the money intended for one bill to pay for another. What I did was use my mortgage payment to keep the heating on in my home leaving me with no money to pay the mortgage.

Unfortunately it didn't work like that; one thing I have learned if we always juggle with our household expenditure like this, the result will always be the same.

At this point I considered taking a third job but I couldn't find any work. Neither of my employers could offer overtime; everyone was cutting back since the economy was taking a nosedive.

I went through all my expenditures and contemplated ways I could save money but there wasn't much to save. We didn't drink alcohol, smoke, gamble, or go out for meals so I was at a loss. I couldn't work out what else there was to save money on.

Every day I would go to work so stressed that I would have a nap in my car during my lunch hour. I was losing weight and my appetite was so minimal that most days I just stayed hungry so that Nazia and Omar could have extra food.

I spent each night thinking of ideas to generate more income to clear my debts. Nazia asked if everything was okay and I told her it was. I didn't want her to worry about anything because she was pregnant again and the last thing I wanted was to make her anxious.

CHAPTER SIXTEEN

Trying Times

My first child was almost ten months old and was learning how to crawl; it wasn't long before he was crawling from one room to the next playing with whatever he could find. I came home from work one day and ran myself a bath; my back was hurting from standing all day. I left the hot water running and left the bathroom for what seemed like moments. As I left to get some towels, my son crawled in and ran his arm under the scolding hot water thinking he was playing the same way he did when he had a bath. He completely burned his arm so that within minutes the skin was peeling. I quickly wrapped him in a blanket and took him to hospital.

He was crying hysterically and Nazia was extremely distressed. The doctors and nurses attended to him and were simply amazing at making him as comfortable as possible. I was getting even more stressed; I couldn't work out why all of these bad times had come upon us.

In life our thoughts determine what we attract. If your thoughts attract the bad things then that is what you'll

receive. Some of you will be familiar with the law of attraction; whatever your mind thinks about, it attracts.

This is not something I was familiar with back then; I just kept asking God why this was happening to me. I had faith even during the darkest days and I would ask God for the answers.

My father once told me that when you're at school, you're taught lessons and then given tests. In life, you're given tests, which teach you the lessons.

Perhaps what I was going through was a test to see if I could handle what was being thrown at me. It was as if my strength was being built up no doubt in preparation for bigger struggles that I had yet to face.

We brought our son home; he was all bandaged up and the doctors gave him a sedative to put him to sleep so he forgot about the pain. The next morning he got up and crawled all over the place like nothing had happened.

CHAPTER SEVENTEEN

The Tough Times Build Your Strength

It was December 1991 and winter was just around the corner. It was getting colder which meant we had to spend a lot more money heating our home. With a young baby at home and a new baby on the way I couldn't let my wife and child freeze.

There will be countless times when you feel that you no longer have control over your choices; at times like this we blame our circumstances for the decisions we make. We accept that our situation may never change. This is something I did at the time without realising that I could have made better choices, like asking my father for help. I chose not to do that; this decision was my responsibility.

In life if you're responsible, you'll take responsibility for your actions, good or bad. If you're irresponsible then you'll look for something or someone to blame.

My relationship with my father was improving and he was coming to my house to pick up my son and take him out for walks. Nazia was extremely grateful for the breaks because my son could be quite a handful at times. My father would walk four miles to our house and then take my son for a long walk before dropping him back, then walking the four miles home. My father was sixty-nine years old so it was quite an achievement that he managed this two to three times a week.

Meanwhile work was getting more stressful because my employer was struggling with the recession and the bank was putting a lot of pressure on him to reduce his borrowing. If he didn't find another bank his business would have to close and everyone would lose their jobs.

Luckily he managed to get another bank to back his company and they offered him more money to use as working capital to keep his business afloat. I knew nothing about business banking at that age. I barely knew how to manage my own finances let alone how to manage business finances. My only concern was whether or not I had a job.

I worked hard, I made sure I was on time and I did more than what was required of me so I was promoted to area manager. Finally I felt like I was getting a break and the new job meant extra money, which I could use to clear up my debts and get back on track. What I didn't realise was, the more money I earned, the more tax I had to pay. I thought I would have more cash coming in, but it turned out to be much less.

Sometimes a better job that pays more money may not solve your problems. This is something most people believe but unfortunately it is not always the case. I became annoyed as I was working almost day and night, and the taxman was getting all of my money as though he were my employer and kept all of my earnings.

The extra money I was earning was going to the arrears of my bills and my mortgage payments. By the time the bank added on a late payment charge the extra money I was paying only covered the added charges and not the overdue amount.

One of the first things I did was speak to the bank about this issue. I explained that if they kept applying charges I would never be able to clear the arrears. The bank told me that they had no control over it; the terms were clearly noted in my mortgage's terms and conditions.

CHAPTER EIGHTEEN

A Leap of Faith

It was January 1992, and the temperature was below freezing. My heating bills were rising fast and were costing me more than I was earning. I asked Nazia to stay in one room of the house and keep just that room warm by switching the heating off in the other rooms. This only worked for a short while as my son was one year old and wanted to explore the house. Anytime he opened the door the cold air from the rest of the house rushed in.

I didn't know what to do. I couldn't even change to a cheaper supplier because I was behind on my payments with the current one. My credit rating was so poor that I couldn't even apply for a personal loan.

Most people think that debt consolidation loans are the answer. Unfortunately they're only a temporary reprieve because the fact is your debt situation will not change and it will get drawn out over a longer time period, even though you're paying less monthly.

It wasn't just me who was struggling financially; my employer was also stressed and a month later I got laid off from work. I didn't know what to say or do. I certainly didn't want to worry Nazia since she was eight weeks away from giving birth.

How do I keep the roof over my head and provide food for my children without an income?

I went to the state office to claim benefits. I could claim welfare since I was out of work. I'd never been one to sponge off of the state; it was my first time making a claim.

The state office informed me that I could receive weekly support but wouldn't be able to receive mortgage support for twenty-six weeks due to government legislation. I was shocked; at this rate I would end up homeless. They said that if I became homeless they could provide my family with shelter accommodation while they found us lodgings. Such nonsense!

You may feel overwhelmed at times. However over time I realised that the more time I spent blaming others, the less time I had to rectify my own situation.

Every test in our life makes us bitter or better. Every problem can either break us or make us. The choice is yours; you can become a VICTIM or a VICTOR.

I had to take a step back, inhale and remember who I was. I realised I had dealt with difficult situations in the past so I should be able to handle this too.

My father was a wise man so I decided to go to him for advice. I would just tell him that I'd lost my job and leave out my other problems.

He told me that you're never given anything in this world that you cannot handle. He said to be strong, flexible and love others as well as yourself because this will keep you moving forward. Don't be afraid. No one lives

forever, so you just have to live. Refuse to give in to the pain because the energy it takes to hang on is holding you back from new things happening in your life.

I was amazed. I looked up to my father and respected him although I never gave him the respect he deserved. He told me about days when he'd been beaten down and told me how he'd managed to get back up.

Failure happens to the person who stays down. Even if you make one small change at a time, over time these small changes will add up to a create a big transformation, so don't give up.

I managed to get some part time work in a restaurant; the money wasn't great, but it was something rather than nothing. Fortunately I was able to claim some benefits but I still didn't have enough money to make ends meet.

I carried on like this for another two months. In April 1992 Nazia gave birth to my daughter Anah. It seemed like I had the perfect family. Any gentleman would be proud of but sadly all the stress and worry I felt about our financial situation took the shine away from her birth. Nazia and Anah came home a few days later and Anah had a difficult time sleeping at night.

We took Anah to the doctors to be told that she had colic. We were advised to change her baby formula to see if that made a difference.

A few months passed and I had no luck finding full-time employment. I wasn't getting any help with my mortgage either so my arrears just kept mounting up. It was summer so I didn't have to use the heating, which was a relief.

Anytime we heard a knock on the door we stayed quiet and pretended we weren't home, as the only people who came to our door were debt collectors.

I was ignoring the situation, which is something many people do. It's not uncommon for people to think they can just run away from their problems, but the truth is, troubles will find them wherever they are.

I spent a lot of time with my father having conversations about life in general. He was giving me advice and I'd never been good at receiving advice; I was arrogant and thought I knew it all.

No matter who you are, everyone can learn from someone who has experienced what you're going through. They can pass on knowledge and share that experience. You have an opportunity to learn from them; don't let it pass you by.

One day I received a notice stating that my electricity and gas would be cut off. As usual I ignored it. I figured that they couldn't get into the house so they couldn't carry out their threat. What I didn't know was that they had right of access which meant that they could break into my home if they had to.

Time passed by quickly. Every morning the minute I woke up I would worry about how I was going to get through the day and wonder who would be knocking on the door asking for money.

Roughly a week later, the doorbell rang but I didn't answer it hoping they would go away. Sadly they kept ringing and eventually I came out of my room and opened the door.

The man said he had a warrant to cut off the electricity and gas. I explained that I was struggling financially and I was unable to make the payments. I explained that I had two babies at home and that if he cut off my gas and electricity, I wouldn't be able to keep them warm at night or have any hot water.

He was sympathetic about my situation and called his manager who informed him that if I signed a form they could setup prepayment meters in my home for my electricity and gas. This way it wouldn't get cut off. I had no choice so I signed it and let them install the meters. However they didn't tell me that my arrears would be uploaded to the meter to be deducted at a set rate.

This meant that for every £10 ($15) I paid into the meter, approximately £7 ($10) went toward my arrears and left us with around £3 ($5) to power our home. Some days we didn't have enough money; I didn't top up the meter and we went without power. It didn't matter though as the debt kept being added to the meter so every penny I paid was swallowed up.

Finally I gave in and went to my father for financial help. He loaned me some money from the little savings he had; he'd been keeping it by for a rainy day. I used it to pay off a proportion of my electricity and gas bill. This at least assured me that I could keep the lights on for longer periods of time.

My kids were growing up fast and required bigger clothes and more food. I didn't have any money so most days Nazia and I went hungry so that our children could eat. It was awful, especially for Nazia. My intention was to never put her through such hardship; seeing her sad or upset would make me cry at night. Nazia seemed tougher than me and never let anything get to her, whereas I just kept wondering when this situation was going to improve. Each day felt like a new challenge.

I took action and decided to study computer programming. The government provided free training. Unfortunately it was almost four miles away from home and since I couldn't afford the bus or train fare, I just got up early and walked.

It was good to be out doing something and mixing with other people who were looking for work and facing similar challenges to me. I was a fast learner and picked up how to program computers quickly. I am an expert at programming today having used computers for over twenty years. My aim was to get the qualification then start applying for jobs in that field.

Sometimes, you just need to take that leap of faith. We need to get knocked down, so that we can learn how to hold our position in the arena of life.

Most people don't get out into the arena of life because they don't want to fight, or have a fall.

Life will, at some point, knock you down, whether you're on the field or sitting on the sidelines, so at least get knocked down for following your dreams.

This was one of the reasons I took a risk on the training course. I believed that given the struggle I was going through, if I stayed at home worrying I wouldn't be helping my situation or myself.

When I came home I was exhausted from the walk and the ten hours spent at the training centre. However, I am the type of person who can work long hours without complaint.

CHAPTER NINETEEN

Eviction and Loss

Winter was upon us again. It was November 1992 and I celebrated my twenty-first birthday at home with Nazia. She gave me a letter, which she'd to sign for earlier that day. It was an eviction notice from the bank. I didn't even read it fully since I knew it was coming. I figured that I no longer needed to pay the mortgage if they were taking back the property.

So Nazia and I had little money and winter had kicked in. Any money I did have went toward heating our house and making sure the children were warm and fed.

I went to see my father but I never told him about my situation. I just went to see him because I missed him and the thought of being with him provided me with great comfort. We got chatting; he talked about the fact he was getting older and that it wouldn't be long before his time was at an end. I told him not to be silly as he'd likely outlive me. He said that if anything happened to him, I had to look after my sisters. I told him to change the subject since it wasn't something we needed to worry about right then.

I left wondering why my father was saying such things so on my way home I brushed it aside. With the problems facing me it was something I didn't need to think about in much detail.

My eviction date was set for the fourteenth of December 1992. A week or so before our eviction I was so broke that I had no money to buy food. It was my fourth or fifth day of being hungry but I made sure that Nazia and the children ate and I just pretended to be on a diet.

One afternoon I searched my house for money and discovered a box full of copper coins. I counted them out; the total came to about £7 ($10) which was enough to buy nappies and baby milk.

I went to the store and explained to the shopkeeper Ahmed, I needed formula and nappies but all that I had was a box full of copper coins. I apologised and told him that I desperately needed these items for my children. Ahmed returned the box of coins to me and told me to take whatever I needed. That same shopkeeper is still a close friend twenty plus years later. I will never forget anyone who was there for me during my time of need.

On the night before the fourteenth of December 1992 my family was all packed up with whatever essentials we had. It was our last day in our home. I had arranged accommodation for us at a homeless unit as I couldn't go back home to face the music with my father. I knew in my heart that it wouldn't be long before I was back on my feet and I could put all this behind me.

After the eviction I went back to my training course. Later that afternoon at around two-thirty pm, I received a call from my stepsister Parveen's husband to say that my father had had a heart attack and passed away.

My first reaction was is this a joke? If it was, then it was a pretty sick one, but I knew Parveen's husband Amin was a serious man and he rarely joked about anything. I was speechless with anguish.

I was so broke that I couldn't afford the bus fare to go to see my dead father's body. I had to walk six miles to the hospital in the freezing snow. When I arrived I was taken to the family room to have a chat with the doctor who explained what had happened to my father. He said that there was a delay in the ambulance reaching him. I was so angry; I thought if only they'd reached him in time then he would be alive. But I was only looking for someone to blame.

Muslim tradition states that the burial must take place quickly but I was so broke that I couldn't pay for his funeral. I sought help from the local mosque, which covered the funeral costs using its community fund. I could pay this back once my father's estate was settled.

The day couldn't have gotten any worse for me; I'd been evicted from my home in the morning and my father had passed away in the afternoon. I kept wondering why God hated me so much that he would put me through such pain and misery.

In life, you'll realise that you'll have to face challenges. When you decide to face them, you will gain strength, confidence and courage. Only then can you say, I have lived through this horror and survived.

CHAPTER TWENTY

The Road to Recovery

Losing my father was difficult because his death was sudden and I'd never imagined it happening. Nazia and I moved back into my father's house as my younger sister Shabana was alone. Everyone in the family was in shock due to my father's passing; I thought he would outlive me but life isn't like that.

My main focus after losing my father was to get back on my feet. I'd lived through everything that life had to throw at me and I was determined that I would make it back.

As children, we are programmed to believe that something or someone is responsible for our lives, but the harsh reality is everything we ever hope to achieve is up to us. The only question you need to ask yourself is this: "What are you going to do about it?"

I could sell anything; this was a skill I knew I had from my days working on the market stalls. All I needed was something to sell and to not pay for the products upfront.

I finished my computing training course and in 1993 mobile phones were gaining popularity in the marketplace and everyone was looking to buy one. I just needed to come up with a way to build stock and then find the customers.

I went to numerous mobile phone stores to ask if they needed anyone to sell their products for them. I wasn't looking for employment although most stores thought I was. I explained that I would purchase the phones at cost to sell them under a contract and we'd split the commission fifty-fifty. If I didn't sell anything, they'd lose nothing. There were a few telecom providers who had their own retailers at the time so I did the same at every provider's store, which allowed me to give my customers a choice of phones and networks.

When you're selling a product, write a list of reasons why a customer wouldn't want to buy that product. Spend time studying your objection handling techniques. The more you study how the sales process works, the more you will sell. Bear in mind that usually people buy things based on emotion, not logic.

I asked the stores to let me spend a few days with them to learn about the product and shadow their best sales guys. It would have been stupid not to allow me to do so since I knew I could make more money for them than all their sales staff combined.

A bold claim, but if you don't believe it, how can you achieve it?

Many people don't believe they are capable of anything they set their mind to; they normally need to see it to believe it. This is the completely the wrong approach because if you believe it, you'll see it

I needed money for leaflets. If I could get around ten-thousand leaflets printed then I could target areas where people are most likely to buy mobile phones. I couldn't fund the leaflets myself so I used my charm to convince the retailers to pay for it. I knew that if I got one hundred customers to sign up, that was more than the stores would have gotten in a year.

It wasn't easy; I was spending long solitary hours every day going up and down stairs posting leaflets under people's front doors. My target was to hit a thousand homes a day. I would not rest until I finished even if it took me until midnight.

After a few days I was getting calls and messages. My sister answered the calls and told people that one of our sales representatives would get back to them. The customer didn't know I was a one-man band. During one day I received almost ten calls. The first thing I did was book appointments with these customers. I visited them at home with samples of the handsets, which were made from clay. After they saw all the different designs I would match them with the best handset based on their practical and stylistic needs. Then I offered them a contract based on their monthly budget.

If I had free time between appointments, I would post more leaflets. I didn't want to lose momentum with customer enquiries; juggling this with the appointments was tough and tiring but the adrenaline rush from making sales kept me going.

Sometimes you need to work harder than others to get what you want out of life. Most people aren't willing to

do that. They would rather work eight faithful hours a day. So don't give up because you're working long hours, it won't last forever.

Within a few months I had made over a hundred sales and the retailers couldn't keep up with the amount of contracts I was bringing them. Then I started to receive commission.

I wanted to buy another home for my family and this time I wanted to be sure that I had a really big deposit so I wouldn't struggle with mortgage payments like before. Since I was working toward a goal, the long hours delivering leaflets and attending my appointments didn't faze me in the slightest.

I was making more money at twenty-two working for myself than I ever did working for an employer. It wasn't long before I had managed to earn the money I needed to buy a house.

Once I'd finished a day's work, Nazia and I would walk through different neighbourhoods viewing houses and tell ourselves that we would love to live in the area one day.

Most people will never do that. They'll never view the house of their dreams, or sit in a car they would love to drive, or pick up a brochure about their dream vacation. Why not? Simply because they don't believe they will ever achieve it and they don't want to chase their goals because of the fear of failure.

As a child, my dreams were to become a pilot, drive a fast car, have a big house with a garden and travel the world. At no time did I ever think that any of that was impossible. I just knew I would make it happen, so I envisioned the house

I would buy or the car I would drive or the places I would visit someday. It gave me hope that someday it would come to pass. I figure that if people aren't laughing at your dreams and goals then you have not set them high enough.

Keep in mind that you'll achieve more in the future than you will have lost in the past. In life, there will be winners and there will be losers. There are even people who just haven't learned to win; this is something I hope to teach you.

Late one night I'd finished my appointments. I hadn't been spending much time with Nazia and the children because of the long hours I'd been working. I was lucky that Nazia understood why I working those long hours. Nazia understood our situation and even though we aren't together today she would keep reminding me that all we needed was each other and that she believed in me. This was what kept me going.

One night we went for a walk and noticed a house for sale in the neighbourhood we wanted to live in. Not only that, it was a three-bedroom house. This meant that my children would be able to have their own rooms.

I couldn't sleep that night because I felt so excited. The next day I made an appointment with the real estate agents to arrange a viewing of the house. I spent the whole day looking at my watch as the appointment was at seven pm. Nazia and I went to view the house together while my sister watched my children. We loved the property and the following morning I put an offer on the house.

CHAPTER TWENTY-ONE

New Chances

My younger sister was soon to be married, so in a lot of ways I had joy in my life. Everything was falling into place and after the struggles that I'd endured over the last few years it was a welcome relief. My father's estate had also been settled and I was in the process of signing over his house to my younger sister so that she could start out with her first home.

I was delighted that my sister was so happy especially since my father had made me promise to look after her before he died. I still look after her today; she means the world to me.

My move in date to my new home was the same day as my sister's wedding. I figured that by the time the wedding was over, we could finally move into our new home and it would be a fresh start for both of us.

I collected the keys to my new home earlier that day and went to see it on my own. When I walked through the front door for the first time, I looked at the house the result of my long hours and hard work and started crying. These were tears of joy; it felt like an emotional release; Nazia and I had overcome all our past struggles.

The greatest enemy of success is the fear of failure and the greatest enemy of progress is your last success. Your future is more important than your past as your future is unlived.

Finally I had purchased another home for my family. Nazia said that she'd always believed in me and that she had prayed to God every day to make sure I went back to being the Tahar she knew who remained a fighter no matter what life threw at him.

We all need to have faith. It doesn't matter what religion you are, whether you follow God or not, it's important to have faith in something. Even if it's just in people or in the universe, it's having faith at all that matters. Faith will get you through anything you might be going through.

Things were going great so I decided to cut back on my working hours and find myself another job. I knew more and more people were flooding the market with all sorts of deals and this time, I wasn't going to get complacent so I made sure my bases were covered.

I didn't want to go back to working for Pakistanis, so I thought I would work for a large-scale corporation. But how would I get my foot in the door?

I phoned a few friends and asked them to notify me of any jobs in the corporate sector so that I could apply for them. A week or so passed and I found a job advertised in insurance with a major bank called TSB. The advert said that no experience was required so I applied for the job.

A few days later I was invited for an interview and attended an assessment day. The other potential candidates and I had to take basic tests that assessed our listening, reading and writing skills. If a candidate passed the tests they would be invited to an interview that afternoon. I passed with flying colours and had about an hour before my interview. A few days earlier, I had learned everything I could about the company just in case I was asked any questions about the organisation.

Today, most companies use a "competency based" interview with new recruits. My personal opinion is that this is a useless interview technique. How does, "give me an example of etc." define how a good an employee a person will to be? Whenever I employ someone, I focus on their entrepreneurial spirit and try to determine their hunger and desire to succeed.

If you own a company and your employees are unhappy, take note of the above. It could be the primary reason your business is unsuccessful today.

I was hungry. I could sell anything; they'd learned this at my interview. A few days later I received a job offer. Since this job was part-time and my mobile phone business was slowing down due to the high level of competition, I looked for weekend work to ensure I was able to afford all of my household expenses. I'd seen a position advertised for Urdu/Punjabi speakers with a company that planned to launch a new Pakistani/Indian television service.

I applied and was called in for an interview. It wasn't really an interview but a single question: could I speak Urdu and Punjabi? Since I was fluent in both I was immediately offered the job. At just twenty-four years old, I was working for two of the largest corporations in the UK.

I was working seven days a week but loved every minute of it. I was gaining knowledge about the corporate world that I never would have learned elsewhere. I was the first person to arrive at work each morning and the last to leave at night. I was hungry to absorb whatever I could about the business and work my way up. If there were extra hours available, I would sign up. I knew that I could learn more with every extra hour spent at work.

In life, give more than the basic requirement, because the more you give, the more you'll get. Even if your employer doesn't acknowledge your efforts, the people around you will come to you for help and advice. Soon you will become the first person they go to for help.

CHAPTER TWENTY-TWO

Chasing Success

The training I received from the bank each week was invaluable; they asked me if I would like to take the Financial Planning Exams at their expense. I agreed as I would be able to work as a qualified financial advisor. I studied for nine months and passed all the exams that I needed to become qualified; I then worked my way up the company.

At my weekend job, I was using the skills I'd learned at the bank and vice versa. Soon I was holding senior management positions in both of these organisations.

I was in such a happy place in both my personal life and professional that I became very focused on succeeding. What really mattered to me was my career. I was both saving and investing money. I bought stocks and shares along with bonds and pension plans, which I'd known nothing about before entering the corporate world.

It was all about developing new abilities and skills to increase my knowledge. I believed that this was my most valuable asset and would determine my earning ability.

Learn new skills that will make you valuable in your current job. If you have the skills an employer requires, this

will determine almost 90% of your earning power. Don't waste your time watching TV, go out there and determine your financial future.

Things couldn't have been going better for me; I finally managed to buy my dream car, a BMW; my days of stealing cars were behind me. I even took my first holiday, which I spent in Tunisia and went on a four-day camel trek in the Sahara Desert.

My children were growing up and were now at school. I couldn't believe how quickly time was passing by. With all the hours I spent working I felt as though I was missing a huge part of their lives. I'd never seen their school plays or even had time to sit down with them and go over their homework or ask them about their day.

My daughter Anah came home once with a picture that she'd drawn in school. She was desperate to show me the picture but I was too busy to even look at it. She proceeded to scream the whole house down. At that point I finally took notice. Most people need to take the small pleasures into account whilst chasing the bigger ones.

The value of life is not in its duration but in its donation.

I'd become so focused on my career I'd forgotten to see what was happening around me.

CHAPTER TWENTY-THREE

Fatherhood and Marriage

I knew I had to make some changes in my life so I cut back on the hours I was working at the bank to spend more time with my children. I took them to and from school, which was something I'd never done before.

I recall the smile on my daughter's face when I picked her up from school; she lit up like a Christmas tree when she saw her daddy waiting at the school entrance. It meant so much to me and I knew that all of this would have been lost if I'd kept focussing on my career.

I spent more time with my children taking them to the park, the zoo, the beach and the swimming pool. The reason I had never done these things with my children before was because my own father had never done any of it with me.

I'd just thought it was normal for a father to go to work and for a mother to take on the responsibility for the home and the children since my father and mother did the same. It was all I knew but life was teaching me new things through my children and I was thankful and blessed for the lessons.

The most significant investment you can make is in your own potential for greatness, so ask yourself these questions: What do you want from life? What do you want from your relationships? Do you have a plan? Do you even recognise your own value? How many mentors and role models are in your life that can help you shape it the way you want it to be?

We all make mistakes; that is a part of life. Einstein once said, "Experience is the name we give to our mistakes." So don't be afraid of making mistakes.

In life we can determine our circumstances; they don't have to determine us.

I was learning how to be a loving father and be there for my children, even if it was only to comfort them.

Learn to appreciate yourself and believe that you have potential and a future; allow yourself to dream of everything that makes you happy. Establish a plan to work toward that dream and take responsibility for your own life. Believe that good things are meant to happen to you.

Spending quality time with my children and family made me realise that my best days were ahead of me. I wanted to enjoy what I had; it's impossible to know when life might throw you another curveball and everything can change in an instant. I learned to enjoy the small things in life without fear getting in the way.

When you expect fear, you're inviting it into your life. Don't give in to fear, because that allows it to become a reality. Many people kill their dreams with negative thoughts, so don't let that be you.

My relationship with my children was improving and as the years passed, I began to realise that I wanted more out of life. I didn't know exactly what I wanted.

At some stage you may question why you are on this planet, and ask yourself things such as: Am I in the right job? Am I with the right person? Am I where I should be, or am I meant for bigger things?

I knew that I was meant for a bigger calling and purpose. I had seen what hardship my father endured and my heart told me to aim high in life but Nazia didn't share the same vision as me. She was a simple woman who was happy with what we had and she didn't desire any more. Nazia believed that more success brings more problems.

Things were changing at the bank. There were new faces in management and even new CEOs who wanted to take the bank in a new direction. Changes would occur at the expense of the employees but I was never fazed by change.

However I did become upset when my colleagues became unhappy with the changes; their attitudes changed from positive to negative. I decided it was time for me to leave this organisation.

I wasn't worried about finding a new job because I was a highly experienced worker with almost four years experience at two of the largest corporate institutions in the United Kingdom. I applied for senior positions at different companies.

Most people will never apply for highly paid jobs simply because they don't believe they could actually get the job. These people fear rejection but don't let it faze you; rejection simply prepares you to aim even higher next time.

Ask yourself this: What is it in your life that stops you from aiming high? The answer to this question will be the key to your inner-strength.

A few weeks later I received a job offer from Prudential, a major employer in the finance sector. It was quite an achievement for me; I was providing financial advisors with quotations for investment products.

I really enjoyed my new career and I was part of a great team. Everyone was positive and happy in the workplace, which was a big change from the environment I had left at the bank.

I wanted to learn as much as possible so I took books home and studied all the products my new employer offered. I learned all of the product details; I wanted to ensure that if someone asked me a question, I would know the answer. It wasn't long before the senior managers noticed how other staff members were always asking me for help and it wasn't long before a new position became vacant for an account manager in national accounts.

Instead of applying for this position, I was approached by a manager called Jo Page. Jo won my instant respect and admiration when she considered me for the role, mostly for believing I was capable of doing the job.

The human mind has the potential for so many things. Learn to stand up to any negative thoughts and short circuit that cycle of negativity by talking positively to yourself.

It was a great opportunity and I was offered the job after the interview. I went home to tell Nazia the good news but she didn't share my enthusiasm. Nazia wasn't interested in my career as she knew how I was changing as a person. I was focusing on my career instead of my family. That killed the joy for me; as I'd worked so hard to provide for my family.

I realized that we had gotten married so young; we were starting to grow apart. I wasn't going to be satisfied staying in the same place all my life like my father had done. I wanted to go further and set new standards for myself using my newly acquired talents and abilities. Nazia and I started to become distant with one another.

I wished my father were here, as I knew he would have had the answers and given me the best advice about what to do in my marriage. It was at times like this that I wished I hadn't let the advice he'd given me go in one ear and out the other.

Ask elders what they wish they had accomplished in their lives. This will give you some insight into their unfulfilled potential.

I loved my job at Prudential; the people there were "hungry" to make money and succeed which was something I embraced. I began earning between £10,000 ($15,000) and £15,000 ($22,500) a month in salary and bonuses.

In 2000, I was twenty-nine years old and earning this type of money. It was way beyond anything I'd ever dreamed. I wasn't complaining. I worked even harder, spent more hours at work and travelled the country to meet with clients and build relationships. I ended up being one of the top ten performers for the company.

This was quite an achievement for me. I came home one day to show Nazia the list of top ten performers and where I was on it but she wasn't interested. She hardly understood what I did and if anyone asked her what I did for a living, she'd tell them that I worked in an office.

When you prepare for lift-off, the first thing you do is fasten your seatbelt and brace yourself for turbulence.

I was flying high but my marriage was experiencing severe turbulence. I would come home from work and immediately begin arguing with Nazia. My children would get caught up in the fighting, something I vowed would never happen especially considering I grew up with parents who never even spoke to one another.

What was I doing wrong? I worked hard, provided for my family, ensured we kept a roof over our heads and meals on the table.

I wanted the best for all of us but Nazia said she that didn't know who I was anymore. She told me I was so engrossed in the corporate world earning money with materialistic people, that I had forgotten who I used to be, a person who valued the real things.

Perhaps she was right. Had money gone to my head? Was I becoming someone I wasn't?

I had been accused of being stubborn, selfish and arrogant. Was this really me and who I had become?

I disagreed mostly due to pride but perhaps the stark reality was staring me in the face and I was just too blind to see it.

I'd spent the last ten years on such a long road to recovery struggling with the constant arguments at home, which greatly upset my children so I finally decided that enough was enough and that it was time for me and Nazia to take some time apart.

She was devastated that I could even contemplate such a decision. Nazia was born in Pakistan with a different cultural upbringing than those of us brought up in the west. She was taught that no matter what happens in your marriage you stick it out to the end.

But I'd found my own place and the day came when I had to leave my marital home and children. Walking out on my children albeit for the best was the toughest thing I'd ever had to endure. It broke their hearts and they kept crying and clinging to me saying, please don't leave daddy.

CHAPTER TWENTY-FOUR

Interfering People

I had left home with just my clothes and moved into an empty apartment on the south side of Glasgow about three miles from my children. The only positive thing about the situation was that I would be close to them.

That first night I slept on the floor with the heating on. I only had a jacket to keep me warm. Fortunately I did have the funds to buy myself the essentials I needed.

I went to work the next day but didn't tell anyone that I had moved out. I buried myself in my work, which kept my mind occupied. I would still see my children almost daily because I picked them up each morning to drop them off at school before I left for work. It lifted my spirits knowing that they didn't have to watch their mum and dad fight every day.

There will come a time where you have to go within yourself, simply to build strength. This will give you some clarity on the decisions you have made.

This is what I was doing; the more I thought about it, the more I felt I had made the right decision.

However it was not long before Nazia approached my aunts and uncles. She asked them to speak to me about coming back home. Being born into an Asian community can sometimes be very difficult; it can feel as though other people dictate the choices you make in your life. I stood my ground as my view has always been the same...

Other people's opinion of you is none of your business.

Where were these people when I didn't have a penny to my name and when I'd not eaten in days so that my children could eat? Where were these people when I needed nappies and milk for my children? Where were these people when I had to walk 6 miles in the freezing cold snow to see my dead father? Where were these people when the Sheriff Officers were evicting me from my home?

I'll tell you where they were...nowhere to be seen!

So how dare they tell me how to live my life! I respect my elders because that is what my father taught me to do. So I was never rude or abrupt to them but my reply remained the same...

I cared what people thought about me until one day, I tried to pay the bills with their opinions.

If you are in the same situation now, read the above message repeatedly; it will make you take stock of your life as it did mine.

During the worst times of your life, you get to see the true colours of the people who say they care about you.

CHAPTER TWENTY-FIVE

Career Minded

I was enjoying my job and my performance was being noticed. I was proud of what I was achieving because I felt like I was making a difference selling our products.

During the week, I worked at Prudential and on the weekend I continued doing my other job. I never felt tired or considered reducing my hours.

Most people I meet at my talks and seminars hate their jobs. I know how they feel; I have been there myself, so understand completely.

A person should ask the question:

What are you going to do about it?

You're not working for your employer because they like you, you're there because you're doing the job and making things happen. This means that you have the ability to do anything you want to do.

Think about that for a moment. Do fear, limited vision and lack of self-esteem keep you from doing the things you most want to do?

Throughout my career there have been days when I've hated going into work on a Monday morning. I would start feeling sick on the Sunday afternoon because I knew I had to be at work the next day. Some Mondays I would drive past my workplace as I could not even face going in. I came back though because I had bills to pay.

CHAPTER TWENTY-SIX

Living the High Life

I was a year away from my thirtieth birthday, which seemed like quite a milestone for me. I'd never forgotten where I came from, a young boy who had worked at the market selling jeans and computer games to working at two of the largest corporate organisations in the UK.

I was learning more and more about investing money. I was also buying property to rent out, which provided me with an additional income. I wasn't greedy; I just wanted to build a decent portfolio so that I could retire early. I wanted to make sure that my family would have enough money for my funeral and not be in the same situation I was in with my father's funeral.

Things were going well and I had a good relationship with my children. There were no more arguments between their mother and I and I loved both of my jobs.

I had now acquired a few properties and I was earning a good income from them. I invested the money in additional properties.

I never believed that I would be investing in property portfolios. I did what most people do; anything I earned would pay my bills and anything left over would be spent.

The majority of us live like this, me included. We all want nice things and we're willing to live beyond our means in order to have them. Nowadays buying things is so accessible; we think nothing of buying things on credit. Even though I was saving and investing money, I spent the majority of my salary on material things such as a nice big apartment, a fancy car, clothes and holidays.

The way I saw it was, if I was earning, I might as well be spending. I wasn't going to take it with me if I died tomorrow.

What I never thought about was losing my income. How would I pay for all the things that I'd bought on credit or maintain the high lifestyle I had created for myself?

Oscar Wilde was on his deathbed drinking champagne, when his doctor asked him what he was doing. His reply was, "Alas, I am dying beyond my means."

At the time I didn't contemplate the thought of losing my income. I loved having the things I had always dreamed of even if it meant getting into debt in order to have them. The way I looked at it, it was highly unlikely I was going to lose my job so I didn't need to worry about it.

I was foolish thinking that way. The lessons I'd learned about having no money or anything to eat didn't teach me anything. I didn't even notice who I was becoming when I looked in the mirror; I was just someone who felt like he had to keep up appearances.

CHAPTER TWENTY-SEVEN

Losing my Stepsisters

My eldest stepsister Parveen had distanced herself from me a few years previously. Parveen sent Shabana and I a twenty-eight page letter, writing in explicit detail about how she never wanted to see Shabana or me again.

This came as quite a shock as I'd always been extremely close to Parveen. After my mother's death, I saw Parveen as a mother figure. I'd spent so much time with her and helped to raise her children; I didn't want to believe she could write such things. Nevertheless, I had to live with it. She was adamant that she no longer wanted anything to do with me for no obvious reason. I remembered some of the advice that my father used to give me and wished her well.

Shameen on the other hand only spoke to me when she needed money. She was a drug addict and an alcoholic so any money Shameen had would go straight to fund her habit. I still gave her money. Some would say that was the wrong thing to do, but I'd seen how my father used to look out for her before he died, and didn't see why I should be any different. I had no doubt; he would have been looking down on me so I certainly didn't want to disappoint him.

I did tell her that she should come off the drugs and get checked into a rehab centre to clean herself up but her response was always the same: "My life is none of your business."

There is something inside you stronger than the poison you put into your body.

I used to say this to Shameen and any other addict I met who attended my seminars. It's not easy to deal with an addiction of any kind but the true struggle is getting clean.

Tragically, one evening on her way home Shameen was brutally gang raped, had her throat slashed and left for dead.

Miraculously she survived. She was a fighter but the trauma was too much to bear and she took a fatal heroin overdose. For the first time in her life she was at peace and in a better place.

I did not even know until a few weeks later of her passing as Parveen did not even inform me, to this day, I do not even know where she is buried to even pay my respects.

CHAPTER TWENTY-EIGHT

A Great Mentor

I needed to move on from Shameen's tragic death; it was a new year, and I was determined to put the past behind me. My thirtieth birthday was approaching. I returned to work after the break to be informed of substantial changes in performance measurement for every member of staff in the company.

In the previous year I was a top performer. It was obvious that I would be expected to perform even higher this year.

This didn't faze me in any way but we had a new CEO. His nickname was Chopper and he was renowned for cutting staff by the thousands wherever he went.

I'd never really concerned myself with senior office politics so I got on with my job. New employees started at the company. Most of my time was spent at airports, travelling to meet new clients.

I had a great relationship with my line-manager Jo. She was an amazing manager and someone I considered a personal friend. The support I received from her was invaluable as were the lessons she taught me.

Not all managers help people to see themselves as they are. Some managers are leaders who help people see themselves as better than they are.

Jo was like that which was great for me because she spent a lot of time developing each member of our team. Every month she took the team away from the office environment for a face-to-face meeting and asked us what areas we, as individuals, felt that we could improve on or needed help with.

The first quarter passed and I was below my target. It wasn't just me that had fallen below target, a lot of my work colleagues had as well. The market was getting tougher and our competitors were offering the same products cheaper.

When I met with Jo, I could have come up with excuses. Instead I was brave enough to admit that I was struggling.

Being strong, open, and honest is something that will save you in this world.

Life is about expectations. If you expect nothing, you get nothing. My expectation was to increase my performance over the next quarter. I had to program my mind to ensure it would happen.

Success occurs when your dreams become bigger than your excuses.

I had three months, so I sat with Jo and drafted an action plan that would help me to increase my sales figures by the end of the next quarter.

One thing I have learned during my years in business is never set weekly, monthly, quarterly or yearly goals. Always set DAILY goals, no matter what line of work you're in!

The reason for this is simple: if you or your staff has had a bad day, you can easily put it behind you and start over the next day.

When you set monthly goals and someone has a bad week, their level of motivation drops for the rest of that month. The first thing they think is that they will never achieve their monthly goal.

It can be a case of mind over matter. Thinking negatively because you have had a bad week programs your brain the wrong way; this can have catastrophic effects on your ability to achieve your goals and move forward during the rest of the month.

Don't expect to see positive changes in your life if you continually surround yourself with negative thoughts or people.

I would come into work earlier, make more phone calls and study all of my competitors' literature and brochures looking for weaknesses in their products and highlighting these issues with a pen. This way, I was able to respond successfully to objections before my clients even brought them up. By the end of the second quarter I had achieved my target.

Here is a small fact for you; in any sales job only twenty percent of the sales staff makes eighty percent of the money.

The third quarter had arrived and I had to up my game since it was the period most of my clients would be on holiday; this would have a drastic effect on my sales figures.

This meant that I had to get double the sales to achieve my targets, not a simple task by any means.

Sitting with Jo every month was great because she continued helping me with my action plans and advised me to keep phoning my clients. I got to know them very well and kept a notebook filled with our conversations. I asked about their personal lives, the ages of their children, which football team they supported and where they were going on holiday.

Then I would ask about these things on my follow up calls. I'd ask how someone's mother was after an operation or if their child had started high school and so forth. They were blown away at how much I remembered and it meant a lot to them. It was something that my competitors certainly weren't doing. If you work in sales, I advise you get to know your customers; your retention rate will always be high.

CHAPTER TWENTY-NINE

A Global Crisis

When September 1ˢᵗ 2001 came around, I was below target. I had finished my face-to-face meeting with Jo, who was offering me further support to get back on track.

Everything went well for the first ten days of the month, but on September 11ᵗʰ 2001, a huge tragedy struck the entire financial world and put everything under a black cloud.

Nobody had ever contemplated something as horrific as this happening, or the loss of so many lives. No one could even think about business because they were so engrossed in the news. The world practically came to a standstill.

The company that I worked for sold financial services and products linked to the stock market, so because Wall Street had ceased trading, in case there was stock manipulation going on during the crisis, it caused chaos for our investors, who were nervous about what would happen to their funds.

Trading stopped for four days; this was the longest the NYSE had ever closed.

My bonus was based on targets monitored between the 1ˢᵗ of January and the 31ˢᵗ of December. As long as no clients cancelled their products within this period, I would get to keep any commission I earned.

As you can imagine, everyone at work was in panic mode because most clients cancelled their bonds and investments. They pulled their money out before the market crashed. No one wants to lose the money they have worked hard for and invested.

I panicked as well, and went for the safest option. I withdrew my investments and stock market bonds, and moved this money to a very low interest savings account through my bank.

I was a big risk taker, but even I followed the crowd and copied them.

Don't follow the crowd. You don't know where they're going and neither do they.

I follow this mantra now but I didn't at the time. One could call it inexperience or fear of the unknown; the only thought that crossed my mind was that I couldn't afford to lose the money I had worked so hard for.

Reaching my targets seemed beyond my control. Everyone around me was more or less in the same position, heads down with fear as so many customers were cancelling their products.

By the end of the year I was one of the poorest performers in the league table, which was quite a contrast from the previous year.

CHAPTER THIRTY

Sold Out By a Trusted Mentor

In 2002, there were a lot of changes in the company and the accounts that I was working on in the previous year were all gone. The management was squeezing budgets and it was inevitable that everyone felt under pressure.

Don't fear pressure, for pressure is what turns rough stones into diamonds.

Regrettably this is another thing that I know now, but didn't at the time. Going into work became difficult after 9/11. I felt sick going into work and couldn't wait until I left.

How could this be possible? I loved working here so much that I had given up my weekend job in order to focus all of my attention on this profession.

People around me became despondent, complacent and negative. Naturally if you are surrounded by these attitudes it's very difficult to remain positive.

If you surround yourself with negative or toxic people, chances are you will end up being the same. So I say this: "Surround yourself with people who share your thoughts.

Sometimes being around pessimists is never easy so be close to optimists instead.

Once again I had my monthly face-to-face meeting with Jo; she said that the director wanted to have a meeting with me next week to discuss my sales figures but that it wasn't anything to worry about.

I thought nothing of it. My meeting took place the following week, in a closed room with Jo and the accounts director. I didn't realise that this was actually a disciplinary hearing about my performance; the director pointed this out to me when I entered the room.

This was illegal however I didn't know employment laws at the time, which stated that an employer has to inform their employee of the disciplinary hearing in writing, before it takes place so that the employee has the opportunity to defend himself and take a representative to the hearing.

Jo had lied to me by saying it was a meeting to discuss my performance. I was dumbstruck and in shock so I didn't even take in whatever bullshit he was spouting.

All I remember was the director told me I had two options. The first was to resign and receive a month's severance pay with a satisfactory employment reference. The second option was that I would be brought forward for a disciplinary process for poor performance for termination of my employment; this would be swift with no offer of severance pay or an employment reference.

This didn't leave me with many choices. I was asked to fetch my belongings, go home and think over my options then hand in my resignation since this would be best for all parties concerned.

At the time I wasn't even fussed about being sent home, or what the director had told me; it was constructive dismissal, which I took legal action for later. However, the one thing that truly shocked me at this meeting was Jo.

I had looked up to her, respected her, but even more than that, I had trusted her.

Being subjected to such a tirade from the director didn't bother me; his asking me to resign from the company I loved didn't bother me either. What bothered me most was Jo not saying a single word on my behalf.

Words cannot describe how I felt about this; it was as if someone had drilled a knife through my heart then twisted it to make sure it cut deeply. This hurt me like I had never been hurt before. I realised for the first time in the corporate arena that Jo had hung me out to dry and didn't have my back.

CHAPTER THIRTY-ONE

Taking a Leap of Faith

Without a job, I had time to think about what I was going to do with my life. This time, I didn't have to worry about not having an income because I had enough money to keep me covered for at least a year.

One part of me was still in pain after what Jo had done, but the other part was saying that everything happens for a reason.

I decided I needed a break and went on holiday to Dubai. While I was there, I was like that same kid who used to observe everything that went on in the markets; I watched people running their businesses. I was fascinated by the culture, and how the country had a plan to develop itself into a major tourist destination. Dubai was a tax-free haven, and everyone seemed happy wherever I looked; the country was flourishing as a result.

I was certain now that I didn't want to work for anyone again. I decided it was time to venture out on my own.

In Dubai, I found out that the government now allowed foreign nationals to buy property freehold in the country. I did not have information about property sales or renting but luckily for me, I had a close friend Mack in the United Kingdom who did.

All I needed was the courage to take a leap of faith and believe in myself so that I could start my own business.

So many people get caught up in the pain and misery of life and forget to see the beauty in it. Most of us go through life living a lie or pretending that we are happy and content. If you decide to take a leap of faith, you will be able to handle any challenges you face.

I asked Mack who had a property and letting agency if I could come and work for him. I told him that I didn't want a salary. I only wanted to work for a few months to understand how property sales and rentals worked. Mack said he would speak to his business partners and get back to me. When Mack contacted me, he introduced me to his two business partners.

This was the opportunity I needed in the property industry. I wanted to learn everything about property sales and letting possible in the space of six months. Again, I was going home with all the materials I needed to study. I read up on tenancy laws, and even rights and regulations until I was ready to venture on my own.

With every experience, you will gain strength, confidence and courage, which will help you to do the things you, must do to succeed.

I had to work for free for six months. I looked at the bigger picture; I was working to become my own man.

As human beings we are designed to achieve our goals. When you're not on the right path, developing and growing or being more productive and effective, your life will become be more depressing.

To make things work in Dubai, I would need an income; my set up costs were quite substantial because Dubai has a policy where you must pay twelve month's rent in one lump sum. In 2014, an average two-bedroom apartment for let in Dubai was approx. £31,000 ($45,000).

While I was working with Mack I ran a business online. Most people have seen or used eBay, however it was fairly new back then and I had discovered it one day whilst browsing online. I needed an income to help with the bills and this was an outlet I could use to sell avoiding the huge set up costs of having a storefront. My sister Shabana had gone on holiday to Turkey and met some wholesalers who sold bags, shoes and belts. My sister wasn't very good with computers, so I told her I could help her sell the items on eBay for a percentage of the profits while she ordered and dispatched the items.

Your earning ability is one of your biggest assets. So learn skills that make you money.

Mastering eBay wasn't that difficult and it wasn't long before I was earning healthy revenue per month from online sales. It certainly wasn't the same level of income I was used to earning but I didn't have the headache of having a boss tell me what to do.

During the six months I worked with Mack for free, I had saved up enough money from eBay sales to get back out to Dubai and start selling freehold property.

CHAPTER THIRTY-TWO

Making a Name in Dubai

I went back to Dubai in May 2003. As soon as I landed, I was struggling to cope with the ridiculous temperatures of approximately forty-seven degrees Celsius. It was impossible to walk anywhere without sweating and it certainly didn't help that I didn't have a car; I had to take taxis everywhere.

This wasn't something I'd factored into my budget before I left the United Kingdom.

After all, the last thing a professional wants to do is to turn up to a property viewing in a taxi. It doesn't give a professional much credibility as a sales agent, so I hired a car and driver instead.

I discovered that there were so many freelance agents selling property in Dubai, there was very little regulation of the market, which meant an agent was free to do anything. I've made plenty of mistakes in business, more than I can count, but now I was making way too many.

Don't be afraid to make mistakes as costly as they may be, because your best teacher is your last mistake.

The issue for me was the developers who had over one hundred people selling the same product. This was a nightmare, as it was impossible to know if the property had actually been sold without constantly phoning the developers' office to check.

I was beginning to doubt myself and my own abilities. I realised that I was swimming with some very big sharks in Dubai.

Doubt has killed more people's dreams than failure ever will.

I had to come up with a new strategy or I would end up losing all the money I had saved before coming to Dubai. I noticed that my savings were quickly depleting; I hadn't made money from a single property sale in almost a month.

The property market was booming and prices were rising faster than the developers were releasing properties; the demand outstripped the supply. I should have been able to sell at least one property in this crazy market. The one sale would have given me a considerable amount of commission.

Sometimes, you need to work out what you can do differently from other sellers, so that what you do is unique! This is where the term USP (Unique Selling Point) comes from.

I had to find investors who had already bought property in Dubai and were looking to sell that property to make a profit from rising prices in the market.

I didn't want to go back to regular employment under any circumstances, so I had to find a way to make things work out until I achieved my first sale.

I have learned to follow the rule of three P's. Always remain Patient! Persistent! Positive! – Repeat after me: Patient! Persistent! Positive!

Once I started selling, I got an immense feeling of achievement and fulfillment. I loved being able to do something that no one had dared to do before. I always knew the risks and that I could end up losing everything, but I knew that if I kept worrying about that then I would never be able to move forward.

I wanted to give my life meaning. I was sick of being an employee selling out for a weekly salary or being sold out by those close to me.

A study done in America stated that many employees' had heart attacks on a Monday, between 8am to 9am, going to jobs that they hated and were not challenging.

When you're employed, you already know how far you can go; you know how much you are going to earn and what positions are available if you were to get promoted. It's like watching a movie where you already know the ending; this cannot excite anyone for long.

I've never been one to sit on the sidelines so I took the risk with a leap of faith and started running my own business.

Most people need to reprogram their mind to leave behind their negativity and become more positive.

I had made enough money that I decided to come back to the UK and start up my own business here. At first I couldn't decide what field to get into, but as I'd made money in the property market, I felt it would be best to stick with what I knew.

Most of us will always feel unsure about something. I tend to find a very quiet room with no phone or interruptions, just complete silence; I think about what I'm stuck on and try to focus on the solution for a whole sixty minutes.

When I arrived back to the UK, I met up with my best friend Steven. Steven said that he had been speaking to a friend whose brother in law was selling investment property. He suggested that he could arrange an introduction and I might be able to start selling property for them.

I never like to refuse an opportunity, so I said of course. I met with Iftikhar and Ameen who owned a Property Investment Company.

They had a few property developments to sell so I got all of the details and told them I would look through the information and get back to them after I had carried out some research and due diligence on the projects.

Iftikhar called me the very next day to thank me for my time; I really appreciated the sentiment.

The best attitude you can have is that of gratitude. Having no gratitude is like wrapping up a Christmas present but not giving it.

CHAPTER THIRTY-THREE

Entering the UK Property Business

Iftikhar and I are still business partners today; his one sentiment of appreciation stayed with me to this day. We're very close, and I have learned invaluable lessons from him over the past ten plus years; it's impossible to put a price to his teachings.

I met with Iftikhar and we instantly clicked; he gave me a list of the he had available and asked me how many I thought I could sell. I told him I would sell at least fifty units. I could tell he was thinking, "Yeah right." I said I would contact him again soon with the completed reservation forms.

My heart told me that I could easily sell fifty properties. After all, when I'd worked for one of the largest investment companies in the world, I had sales figures of over £258 million ($377million) and fifty units seemed easy.

One thing you'll find throughout your life is that there will be many closed doors. Don't ever lose heart; if a door is closed, there is a much bigger door waiting for you, I assure you.

I had plenty of contacts from my investment days; Independent Financial Advisors, Solicitors, Investors and people who were always looking for property.

It wasn't long before I had made my first few sales; by day three, I had made twenty-seven sales with full reservation forms and cheques. Within seven days, I had fifty-two sales, which bypassed my goal.

When I gave Iftikhar the reservation forms and the cheques, he was completely mind blown; he couldn't believe it. I submitted the invoice for these sales and he said he would settle up with me once every investor had tied their contracts and their cheques had cleared.

Always do your best to keep to your agreements. This isn't always possible but do your best to keep your promises.

Out of the blue I had a call from Mack who still owned his property rental franchise. Mack and I went way back and had a very close relationship. We had worked together for years at my weekend job whilst I worked at the bank and investment company. I'd spent almost eighteen hours a day with him for over ten years travelling together on long journeys to and from our workplace.

You know who you are and who you are meant to be; the truth of knowing that will set you free on this journey called life.

Mack told me that he was thinking of expanding and buying another rental franchise in the west end of Glasgow. He said the owner was retiring and wanted to sell up so he would be taking over an existing business. Mack asked if I wanted to become a partner.

I knew Mack already had Vaj and Mo working with him. I told Mack that I would think about it and asked if I could sit with Vaj and Mo to discuss how the set up would work.

After my meeting with them, I decided to join Mack in his second branch where I would work fulltime. I was still working with Iftikhar doing property investment, which was also growing, extremely well for me. The difference between the two workplaces was that in one environment, I felt like an owner whilst working with Mack, Vaj and Mo, I felt like an employee.

The issue with having too many owners in one business is that everyone wants to do things their own way and eventually nothing gets done. So set clear ground rules beforehand. Define each individual's obligations clearly in a legally written partnership agreement.

However as this was an opportunity for me to establish another business; it had been brought to me for a reason so I worked hard on both the rentals and the investments.

There were advantages in having a rental franchise it had a database of investors at my disposal. I could use the database to market the properties that I was selling with Iftikhar providing us both with additional sales.

In any line of business look at the opportunities laid out in front of you. Most people are too busy trying to survive that they then don't see the opportunities that are in front of them. So don't let that be you.

The investment business was going well. I was selling more property than Iftikhar so he offered me a partnership in his business as well. This wasn't bad; my manager Jo had sold me out a year earlier but here I was now with two businesses of my own. Three if you count the eBay one with my sister.

I enjoyed working with Mack but I had an issue with Vaj. Vaj liked to be the one who set the rules and expected everyone else to follow. His management mentality was similar to that of the people I'd worked for at the Cash & Carry.

If someone had an idea about expanding the business, he would shoot it down in flames before they even had the chance to explain.

Vaj was the kind of individual who, if you wanted a budget to market the business, would respond that it did not warrant the cost. You can't bring customers in or grow your business without spending anything. However, Vaj thought otherwise.

If the business wasn't growing he would blame someone other than himself.

I collected my daughter Anah from school every day and then brought her to the office. She would help me do the filing, send out mail and help me with some general administration tasks. Vaj through Mack asked me how I was helping the business to grow if I was away collecting Anah. He asked if there was any way that I could arrange for someone else to collect Anah from school; Vaj thought it was affecting the business.

I was literally shocked. I asked Mack if he had missed the fact that I opened earlier than I was supposed to and closed later than anyone else.

All of the staff hated working for Vaj, business partners, contractors, everyone. However Vaj was too blind to see it; he thought everyone respected him.

My advice to you is to, do what you know is right; treat people how you'd like to be treated and don't take any shortcuts. Don't try and cheat; you can either pay your dues upfront or pay later. But one way or another, they will have to be paid.

I've sacrificed some of my dreams by doing the right thing rather than taking shortcuts to reach my goals.

Karma has no expiration date.

CHAPTER THIRTY-FOUR

Erasing Negative Influences

While Mack was on holiday in Las Vegas, I messaged him and told him that when he returned, I wanted to have a meeting with him, Vaj and Mo.

I think that Vaj had an issue with me because I was working with Iftikhar and making more money than at the rentals franchise. I was also travelling to Dubai a lot, so he might've felt that I wasn't committed to the business.

Embrace this philosophy: wishing for others what you would wish for yourself.

If you're surrounded by people who are spiteful or jealous of how well you are doing, then remove these people from your life quickly, as their negative energy can burn you to ash.

I kept the meeting as short as possible. Rather than getting into petty arguments, I explained that I had decided to concentrate on my investment business with Iftikhar and resigned. To be honest, I wasn't worried about walking away; this was the best decision I'd ever made.

I focused on my business with Iftikhar and Ameen. Since Iftikhar was like-minded, we always looked at the bigger picture and didn't sweat the small stuff.

I didn't look back now that I had removed all of my negative baggage; I was surrounded with positive people like Iftikhar, so this was all I needed.

Focus more on the people who inspire you than the people who annoy you. You'll get much further.

CHAPTER THIRTY-FIVE

Growing a Business to Businesses

Things were going really well. I was having the time of my life earning good money and learning from the people around me every day.

Don't get me wrong; I was still making mistakes. This is what happens in business and you learn from it, pick yourself back up quickly and get back in the game.

Mistakes are part of life. If you don't make them, you don't learn. If you don't learn, you will never change the way you do things.

Iftikhar, Ameen and I got on well. We all learned from each another. We were doing so well that we decided to re-brand and change our business model so that we could expand.

I was in shock. When I was working with Vaj, he didn't want to spend a single penny on marketing, yet Iftikhar and Ameen wanted to completely re-brand.

Our first priority was building a website, then making brochures and business cards, and then re-branding.

Everything sounded good when we met with people for these services; they all talked a good game about how they could really make our website stand out and expand our company.

However, over the next eighteen months not one organisation delivered on a single promise. We kept changing the companies we were working with; each company blamed the last, claiming that they were the reason nothing was happening for us.

By this point all three of us were stressed. We had spent the best part of hundreds of thousands on different marketing and website companies, with no returns on these investments.

Here is one extremely valuable lesson I learned from this experience: before hiring someone, always get a reference from another successful business in your field and use the same people they do to market their business.

Never hire an unknown company to build your website, do your marketing or do creative design for your company brochures.

You will learn that if someone builds your company website poorly and it goes online, it can take forever to fix.

Even if you start from scratch, the original domain name will still be active, so anything linked to your previous website will show when people use search engines to find your business. Ensure that it is built properly from the start, and hire a proper SEO (Search Engine Optimisation) company to build it BEFORE it goes live.

I was amazed at what I had learned in such a short space of time. I was spending almost every day with Iftikhar, visiting website companies, design companies, marketing companies and SEO Companies. The information they each provided was inconsistent with the last and my brain was getting frazzled.

When you think you are hitting a brick wall or when things are falling apart, they may actually be falling into place.

When you start your own business you will encounter all sorts of obstacles. The biggest is when people close to you tell you to stick to a regular job and avoid all of the hassle.

People who have no goals or ambitions will always do their utmost to ensure that they sabotage yours as well, so don't let that happen.

Eventually we found three companies that actually did what was asked of them. We hired "Mercury Tide" to build our website. The owner was a gentleman called Tamlin Roberts, one of the nicest guys I've ever met; he was like an encyclopedia of web design.

For the rebranding, we found a company called "Ocean 70." It was owned by Alex Stewart and Scott McBride. Scott later left to move overseas.

For our SEO, we hired Big Mouth Media. Simon Heys knew exactly what we were looking for in the market and gave us everything we needed to create a real presence in the marketplace.

Even after all these years, I still remember everyone's names. The reason is simple; I can't forget that they created the brand it is today.

Never forget the people who help and support you if you take a fall. I didn't meet these people by accident, they were meant to cross my path.

CHAPTER THIRTY-SIX

Creating the Company "Clear"

The cost of re-branding was close to £20,000; however, it was still far less than what we had already spent on companies who'd promised us everything, yet given us nothing.

Some individuals starting a new business cannot afford to pay that amount. Later in my book, I will show you ways to obtain the same quality work for less, so don't lose heart.

Iftikhar, Ameen and I all agreed on the brand name "Clear." This was a suggestion from Alex at Ocean 70; our approach to property investment was transparent.

How many times have you looked back on your life and wished that you had done something sooner? How many times have you had an idea, but someone else brought it to the market simply because you were too scared to try?

It happens to us all. I tend not to regret things I did in the past, since these things made me who I am today. I only regret things I haven't done yet.

We now needed a concept that would differentiate us from other property investment companies.

Suddenly an amazing concept came to Iftikhar; he always joked that he never got very many amazing ideas.

The concept Iftikhar came up with was completely crazy. He said that whenever an investor buys a property from us, we should offer the following three things:

Pay the first two years of rent upfront for an investor.

Fully design and furnish the interior of the property, free of charge.

Pay all of the legal costs associated with the purchase.

My first thought was how the heck do we pay for all of this? It was completely unheard of and no one in the market was doing it.

I had the mentality that if someone told me I couldn't do something, I'd tell them to watch me.

Judging a person or their ideas does not define who they are. It defines who you are.

I should have known better than to do that and after a while, I thought about how we could actually make this work.

Once I got my head around his idea, I realised it was a big financial gamble.

I figured that everyone would say, "This is too good to be true" as it had never been done before. We were actually creating a product that was hassle free for any investor.

Think about it for a moment. When you buy a property that you choose to rent out, you face a lot of hurdles while making sure you get a decent return on your investment.

You need to fund it with a mortgage, get the best rates and then furnish it. You also need to find a letting agent who can market the property and obtain a good tenant. By the time someone does move in, you may have lost eight to twelve weeks of income whilst still making your loan payments.

What we were doing was providing a full turnkey service and giving the investor a no void period, no loss of income, a full furniture package with all legal fees taken care of and the best mortgage deals available anywhere on the market.

Iftikhar's idea was so creative that even I had to applaud his genius. However, we still needed to make money.

Iftikhar said the answer was simple. We would pay the investor the appropriate market value rental, but our profit would be generated by giving the properties to senior executives of large corporate companies. At the time we didn't know any corporate companies.

Whenever you are trying to get more business, don't offer a product. Instead, offer something that reduces people's costs and increases their margins.

Most people when setting up a new business are too busy wondering if they have a great product and spend too much time promoting this. They forget that you instead need to be selling an opportunity that can save time and money.

We had something very unique and I had to formulate a sales pitch for it. The Clear brand was something very classy; everything from our website to our brochures to our business cards had the same look and feel.

Whenever you are creating a new business, ensure that your brand conveys the same image and message that you want to communicate to your customers.

I loved everything about our new brand: the colours; the details; and the message. I was really looking forward to selling our new concept. My first step was to ensure that the corporate companies were in place. If we didn't have them on board, it wouldn't be long before we went broke.

Many corporate companies place their senior executives in hotels, which is quite expensive.

I proposed a small brochure aimed at these companies, stating that we could reduce their hotel costs by fifty percent. We would also provide a full concierge of services to their senior executives.

We appreciated these guys were busy and that they had no time to do these things themselves, so we included all of our services in the price of our rental apartments package.

When you are selling a service, the other party will wonder what's in it for them. As long as you provide them with added value, you will have no difficulty making a sale.

Myself, Iftikhar and Ameen had created a package that benefited everyone. This took about nineteen months to shape and we didn't lose more money than we were making. I could have given up but I believed in Iftikhar's idea; a good business takes time to build and I was committed.

Commitment means staying loyal to your word, long after you made the commitment in the first place.

CHAPTER THIRTY-SEVEN

Embracing Transparency and Building a Reputation

We finally managed to secure new projects with the wonderful package we now offered but we didn't get any customers.

Unfortunately this wasn't what I expected. Every customer thought that it must be a scam.

I am a good salesman and even I couldn't convince customers to buy from us. It was back to the drawing board, but I didn't lose heart.

Iftikhar suggested that we meet some marketing companies who might be able to help by giving us a sales strategy to overcome this barrier. I said I would speak to Alex who might be able to point us in the right direction.

When we explained the problem he said within seconds that our package was "Too good to be true." He suggested that we explain to our customers exactly how we made money.

While not very many companies reveal how they turn a profit, he was right because it answered the questions and concerns of our customers.

You may not know all the answers you need to know. Today, we have the Internet to provide us with any information we need; however, sometimes the best answers come from your elders.

Once I had got my head around Alex's recommendation, I had to find a way to explain it clearly so that everyone I talked to would understand.

We had secured new apartments to sell in Scotland. It was ten units in a small town called Dunfermline and we had a certain number of weeks to sell them. I didn't waste any time and started phoning and emailing investors.

Everyone I spoke to was given my card, company brochure and details for the website to obtain trust and credibility in what we did for our customers.

Remember, if you believe in your product, service and brand, any prospective customer will believe in you.

This transparency when selling apartments made an immediate difference; customers loved my honesty and began to trust our model.

People tend to be open to conducting business with others, but they have to trust you.

Iftikhar and I sold these ten apartments in eight days; the developer couldn't believe it. He had a sales office with full time staff that had sold only one property!

We handed him the reservation deposits from the customers, so that he knew we put our money where our mouth was.

I now had to find a solicitor who could carry out all these transactions for us. A big law firm was needed to inspire confidence in our customers and also ensure that everything went smoothly. This was our first project as a newly branded company, so we simply couldn't afford any slip-ups. We selected a firm called Macroberts.

They were brilliant and we had a whole team appointed to us. I then had to find a mortgage consultant who could provide finance for these customers to help them purchase their properties.

Whichever line of business you get into, my advice would always be: employ the best people to work with you and provide the best service. The reason is simple: if people provide you with the best service then you can provide the best service for your customers.

Imagine for a minute that I'd employed poor solicitors and mortgage brokers; our model would have collapsed before it even got off the ground.

We were close to completion and everyone started taking ownership of their properties, but I guessed that a lot of people were worried about being paid the upfront rental.

To help ease this worry, Iftikhar lodged the money with the solicitors in a nominated account so that the customers knew their funds were secure. All they needed to do now was complete their property purchase.

It all went smoothly. I had the apartments' interiors designed and furnished as per our agreement, and was amazed to see the finished product.

The achievement I felt was immense. I took great pleasure in showing the investors their properties and told them that I'd see them in two years' time. I also thanked them for their business.

Iftikhar advised me to ask our customers if they were happy with the service we provided and if they would recommend us to others.

Always ask for feedback in any aspect of your life. Ask the other person to rate you on a scale of one to ten; most people wouldn't dare to ask. If you score below a ten, ask what it would take to get a ten.

You can apply the same principles to your relationship, business, friendship or anything else. Ask what you need to get a ten.

To expand our company, Iftikhar suggested we offer our existing customers £1000 ($1500) if they recommended another successful customer. This was a great idea. The best way to expand is through your existing customers.

Most business people only reward their new customers; why would you do that? If customers have been loyal to you, reward them. What you may lose in the short term, you will gain in the long term. Look after those who have looked after you, it's a simple motto to follow.

The builder who had given us the apartments to sell originally was so impressed with our service that he gave us more. He also contacted other builders he knew and told them about how good we were.

Selling this one project opened a floodgate of new builders contacting us and offering their apartments for us to sell.

Before we knew it, we had not only amassed a massive volume of sales, we had accumulated our very own property portfolios as well.

In every project we sold to our customers, each of us bought an apartment as well. This gave our customers confidence. If our money is good for the project, so is theirs.

By this point I now owned 15 properties and it all began from just an idea, hard work, persistence and patience.

We had now sold over £20million ($30million) worth of property and I was bursting with pride at everything I had achieved.

CHAPTER THIRTY-EIGHT

Expanding into "Clear Lets"

In 2006, I was still in touch with Mack following his split in the business with Vaj.

Mack had gotten married. He still had issues working as an independent franchisee; all sorts of rules and regulations were imposed on him for no apparent reason, which made it harder for him in his workplace.

Starting a franchise is never easy. Always remember that even though you may think you are self-employed, you are still an employee of the franchisor.

Unfortunately his franchisors were looking for any excuse to terminate his agreement. It was convenient that they already had someone lined up to take his place. It turned out to be Vaj.

Mack came to me for advice and I referred him to a solicitor who was a franchising expert. Mack spent a considerable amount of time and money on a legal battle, deciding he wanted to be rid of his franchise.

Sometimes, people can push you so far that they start to chip away at you, piece by piece. The best way to deal with these people is to walk away. If you let them bully

you into submission, they will always come back to bully you some more.

Meanwhile Iftikhar and I were very focused on getting new customers for Clear Investment rather than continuing to sell to the existing ones.

We realised that our investors were landlords; the fastest route to them would always be through rental agents, so we sent out a mailshot to all of them in Scotland with no response.

Not feeling disheartened, I changed my approach and decided to offer the rental agents £1000 ($1500) for every customer they referred; amazing how my phone starting ringing like crazy after that...

Turnover is vanity, profit is sanity, and cash is reality.

I was never a number cruncher; I hated math at school so much that I used to truant and play snooker instead. Numbers are one of the most crucial elements in business, but I hadn't learnt this because I always left them to someone else.

Don't do what I did and rely on someone else. I suggest that you take a course or read educational books and study the areas you are weakest in. This can be the difference between success and failure.

One of my skills today is the ability to look at a business plan and tell you how much money you are going to make or lose within sixty seconds. However, in 2006, if you had asked me to add up 9+2, my answer would have been 13.

I received a call from Mack saying he had left his lettings franchise and asking how I was doing with Clear Investment. I told him things were really well.

He said he wanted to get into business again and asked if I would be interested in setting something up with him.

I asked Mack if he had any new ideas that he wanted to explore, as he only had experience in property sales and rentals. This was the field he seemed most comfortable in, but now he wanted to use the "Clear" branding for this new venture.

This would be a problem as only Iftikhar, Ameen and I held the rights to the brand.

Sometimes fast decisions are the wrong decisions.

My loyalty to Iftikhar meant more than anything. After all, he had brought me into the business when I was nothing and made me his partner. We had worked so hard in creating a company that had a £20 million turnover all from scratch. The "Clear" brand wasn't just going to be given away lightly.

I met with Iftikhar and Ameen to discuss the idea of using the "Clear" name for a new venture that Mack and I wanted to set up. Iftikhar was okay with it as he knew this meant we would now be visible in cities across Scotland, but Ameen was not; he was only looking at his own financial benefits.

I told Mack we could use the "Clear" name as long as we ensured there was no conflict of interest.

We decided to implement a business plan because he wanted to open three offices: one in Fife; one in Aberdeen; and one in Glasgow.

It was quite ambitious to do so at once simply because of the massive cost involved. However, Mack and I are both big risk takers and this was a risk we were willing to take.

Sometimes there are no such things as unrealistic goals, only unrealistic deadlines.

It took us six months to devise a plan and to design the layouts we wanted for the stores. In November 2007, we decided to call the new venture "Clear Lets."

CHAPTER THIRTY-NINE

Mistakes NOT to Make in Business

In January 2008, my priority was finding the right premises for our new venture: "Clear Lets."

Wherever you decide to open your premises, ensure that you select the right location. This is completely crucial to your success.

We'd made the wrong choice with two of the chosen locations, which turned out to be very costly. We also realised that we would require bank funding, so Mack introduced me to some managers at a local bank and we went over our drafted business plan.

The bank seemed very happy with it; they were keen to lend us money for our new venture, which was a massive relief for me.

The one crucial mistake I made was not showing my business plan to Iftikhar; I should have done this because he was and is a really successful entrepreneur.

Never make this mistake. If you know someone who is successful, then go through your business plan with them. The advice they will give you could be invaluable.

Neither me nor Mack had read the terms and conditions of the bank's loan agreement. Had we done so, we would have understood the restrictions the loan put on us.

If you don't have the capital, you will probably require funding. Before you obtain this, I suggest that you hire a solicitor to review the terms. It will be a small premium to pay to avoid costly premiums later.

CHAPTER FORTY

Trying to Run Before We Could Walk

Mack and I found our first store in a town called Kirk-caldy. We'd noticed the store whilst driving by and arranged a viewing. The store itself was massive and was located in a row with other property sales and rental agents. The location was perfect and I was feeling excited that all the hard work looking for the first store was finally over. When I saw the inside of the store, my heart sank as the premises required a lot of reconstruction. Also, it didn't come with planning consent and couldn't be used as an office until we obtained the local authority's permission.

This also proved to be costly and suddenly I felt like a right idiot not having these matters covered.

We decided to lease the store and wait until the planning consent would be granted which could take up to ten weeks, a nerve-racking wait.

One of the conditions set out in the loan agreement was the bank would only release the funding once we had obtained all three stores.

This was quite a burden and my mind just kept thinking, three stores in quick succession is not going to be easy.

The bank could've at least split the loan into three separate installments for each office we opened.

You have probably heard the saying: learn to walk before you run.

Searching for new stores just to obtain our loan was beginning to stress me out.

Another factor was that the property market was slowing down and we seemed to be heading for another recession. This was something I had not seen since 1991 and all the thoughts of the past were coming back to haunt me. I couldn't have picked a worse time to enter into a new venture.

Meanwhile Iftikhar had recently received a new project to sell in Edinburgh the capital of Scotland. This was a big opportunity to obtain some much-needed additional capital.

I knew if I sold these units then there would be no need to apply for any loan and it would avoid the stress of getting into debt.

Whilst I was spending eighteen hours a day searching Scotland for new store locations, Iftikhar and Ameen were also pursuing new ventures of their own and bought a chain of fuel stations. It seemed we all forgot about Clear Investment.

An entrepreneur is always looking for the next opportunity. This is all well and good, but don't forget what your main income provider is.

I began to feel the stress more and more by every passing day. I barely slept because it felt as though I never had enough time to do all the tasks I needed to do. I was even struggling to find time to spend with my family and friends, or to just take a break.

However, I'd set my goals. I had always been the type of person who relentlessly pursues them no matter what the sacrifice.

Even with our hectic schedules, Iftikhar found a new project to sell in Edinburgh. I don't know how but we managed to meet up to discuss a sales approach. We were both excited at the opportunity we had in front of us. We both worked hard to make sure that we sold all of the units, only this time Ameen wanted to structure things differently.

Instead of paying the rentals upfront, Ameen wanted to pay the clients monthly.

My gut feeling was that Ameen had a hidden agenda and alarm bells were ringing in my mind. Clear Investment was cash rich; we didn't need to drip feed these customers every month as we had enough money in the bank to pay them a lump sum.

I had been Ameen and Iftikhar's business partner for a number of years, so I had no reason to doubt Ameen's decision, however my advice would be…

Listen to your gut instinct, especially if it doesn't feel right.

CHAPTER FORTY-ONE

Business Setbacks

I told Mack how Ameen wanted to pay monthly rentals to the investors. He said that something didn't add up and to be mindful of his intentions.

After Iftikhar and I sold the properties in Edinburgh, I spent days working hard furnishing and getting them ready for rental. I felt so relieved to have earned enough money that I didn't need to borrow from the bank.

However, as the planning consent had still not come through, I didn't need the funds so I left them in Clear Investment's company account.

I was so exhausted I would struggle to stay awake while driving around to locate new stores, so I'd have to sleep in my car when I stopped for a break. Eventually after weeks I located our second store in Aberdeen; it also needed major reconstruction. We put down an offer, only this time I managed to negotiate a year of free rent. This gave me the breathing space I needed until the Kirkcaldy office was off the ground.

What was proving to be a struggle to find was the third store; this had to be in Glasgow but sadly there were very few vacant premises in areas next to other sales and rental agents.

A few weeks went by and I still had not heard from the council regarding the planning application for Kirkcaldy and I started to get nervous. I phoned to inquire as to why it had not yet been approved and they informed me that someone had raised an objection to my application.

This was absurd so I lodged an appeal. I could have let this get to me but I let it run its course and within days the planning was approved.

Mack and I had already spoken to a builder who was willing to work for us. Demolition work was new to me and such a daunting experience where I felt way out my depth; I had no idea what materials were needed or how much the timber, plaster, concrete, cement and electrical components would cost.

I was relying on the builder's insight and valuable knowledge. However, unbeknown to me, the materials cost half of what he claimed he was spending. Stupid me agreed to pay a lump sum amount for the work. The other factor was my rent-free period was used up in the three months it took to get planning approved.

When arranging any contractor, agree on a price and get written invoices for everything. If the contractor fails to provide this, do no conduct business with them under any circumstance.

I had a set budget to cover building costs but this had risen to way beyond what I imagined, so I needed to find the shortfall.

There were still other expenses to cover before the first store could open. The largest being the computer equipment as a dedicated server had to be installed that could feed all the offices from one location.

I felt like an ATM machine; every day there was another cost that wasn't anticipated. There was so much outgoing expense before the store had even opened that I started to doubt my ability in how I missed all of these costs. Suddenly the panic kicked in as I realised I was going to need the bank loan after all.

You may not consider everything that is required to open a store. My recommendation is to visit current business owners in your field and get advice. It will save you time but most importantly, it will save you money.

Luckily for me, I was still getting an income from Clear Investment. Iftikhar was busy running the petrol stations and I heard Ameen was off work with some personal medical issues.

I called him to find out how he was doing, but there was no reply so I left a voicemail.

Opening your first store is hard. The positive is that the learning experience prepares you for the second.

The next task was to hire staff. I'd established good contacts with rental agents and had met a lady named Mary who I offered the opportunity to run the company.

I have always been a firm believer in giving a share of your business because I think it contributes to your success. I arranged for Mary to have a basic salary and twenty percent of the profit. Rather than feel like she was an employee, Mary would feel like an owner.

Don't think about what you can get. Consider what you can give.

I also asked Mary to hire her own staff, which saved me a lot of time; this way I could concentrate on other matters.

I still couldn't find a store in Glasgow but I did manage to find one in Dunfermline 15 miles from our first location. I felt having another office in the same county would work better and give a larger presence.

As the office already belonged to a Real Estate Agent, the owners would not write a new lease; they wanted us to take over the existing lease from the current tenant. It was called an assignation, something else I had never heard of. It was extremely complex and messy, and something I would never do again.

CHAPTER FORTY-TWO

Open for Business

In July 2008, the first Clear Lets store was opened. All of the hard work and sleepless nights had paid off and it looked stunning.

Seeing the end result of the hard work come to life on the high street was such an emotional experience that I began to cry; it was happy tears and an immense sense of relief that I made it this far.

The store was operational almost immediately as I gave it stock from Clear Investment. This kept a small stream of income coming in.

I didn't envisage the total expense involved; even though no money had been borrowed from the bank yet, expenses were already accumulating.

Whenever I set up a business plan now, I ensure that for the first twelve months, there will be no income and factor additional working capital into the budget.

The Dunfermline store had now been signed off by the solicitors, so the bank was obliged to release their funding.

Mack and I had to do it all over again. However, I remembered everything I miscalculated from the first store and this knowledge was invaluable.

This time, I hired a builder I knew and purchased all of the building materials directly.

You may not want to do this yourself as you may think it is very time consuming, but by doing so it saved me thousands.

I felt at least I achieved something by opening the second office for less than the first. I didn't feel as much as an idiot. Yes, we all live and learn, but I don't like to be lied to about how much something is going to cost.

I now had the second store of Clear Lets opened. I was exhausted but the adrenaline rush that came from developing the stores kept me going; I felt so alive and loved the buzz and the feeling I got when I saw the end result was phenomenal.

I recruited two staff members for this branch; one was the branch manager and the other was an assistant. During the interview the manager talked a good game, describing how she could bring in loads of customers and help the company grow.

My gut instinct was to not employ her as I felt she was a complete waste of time, but Mack thought she would be good for the business and offered her the role.

CHAPTER FORTY-THREE

Milestones and Betrayal

We were bringing in new properties with our first store with just two members of staff. What I hadn't envisaged however was that if the property portfolio grew, I would also need to hire more employees.

One of the biggest mistakes I made when employing staff was to give non-performers the benefit of the doubt and offer them additional support.

The branch manager Mack hired for the Dunfermline office wasn't performing and I wish I had gotten rid of her sooner. Had she achieved her targets, we would have broken even, but we were behind by almost eight months and I had a lot of catching up to do.

My advice to new business owners would be if someone is not performing, get rid of them and fast. You may have to pay them a small severance but it will be the best money you've ever spent.

Mack and I needed to bring in double the amount of properties, so I decided to work in this branch myself.

It wasn't easy. I was visiting prospective landlords and was doing the viewings for prospective tenants as well. On top of this, I had to come back to the office and catch up on calls and other general duties. Once I had closed the store, I had to visit the first one to find out what was happening there.

One of the biggest challenges a business owner will face is doing everything. At the beginning, it's hard not to as most people don't have enough capital to hire an entire team.

So put in the hours. It doesn't matter whether you work eight hours or twenty; ensure every hour is productive, as this benefits your whole business.

Although access was available to the bank loan funds, I decided to use this money for an opportunity that arose to buy out one of our rental competitors, Kingdom Letting.

The owners were retiring, but they didn't have a high street presence.

Their rentals portfolio was extensive and had been built up over the years. This would have brought us a considerable revenue stream and really allowed us to get established as a big player.

As I was managing our two stores, I asked Mack to handle all of the negotiations surrounding the acquisition of this business. We got a team of accountants and consultants involved in the process to ensure there were nothing missed.

At the same time, Mack found a new store in Glasgow, which was opposite his old workplace.

The shop required a massive amount of work due to a structural building problem.

I told Mack that it was not a good investment because it would really stretch us financially. He was adamant, so he asked his parents to buy the store and rent it back to

Clear Lets, providing them with an investment and a rental income.

The purchase of Kingdom Letting was finalised and terms had been agreed for a sale price. We put a condition in our purchase agreement stating that if we lost twenty per cent of the rentals portfolio within six months of taking over, then a sum of money would be held back. We had to ensure that there would be a return on our investment.

If you are buying an existing business, always hold back a percentage of the purchase price to cover yourself, in case it doesn't provide you with the agreed income.

One condition of the contract was that we had to retain their staff. This wasn't a problem; it would not have made sense to tell them to leave. After all, they knew the customers better than anyone as they had been working there for seven years.

A few weeks later, the purchase for our Glasgow office was complete. This felt like a milestone for us because we had attained our fourth store. This was on top of the acquisition of Kingdom Lettings. I was tired and felt that we were moving too fast; I didn't want to be in such a risky position.

Even as a big risk-taker, I was beginning to question my poor judgment. I considered how we had expanded so quickly in such a short time.

My father had always taught me not to bite off more than I could chew; yet I had ignored this many times throughout my life.

Our expenses were now even higher; we couldn't fund the two stores yet to open so we decided to sell off Aberdeen.

Always look at your business targets, daily, weekly, monthly, quarterly, yearly and focus on your expenditure. If you see an opportunity to reduce costs, don't hesitate.

The mistakes being made were adding costs, not reducing them. Once the deal was concluded, we were able to focus on opening the Glasgow store. The windows were bare so I had posters made showing that a Clear Lets store was coming soon.

Mack's previous franchisor commenced legal action to prevent us from opening the Glasgow store.

It wasn't clear to me why his previous franchisors had done this.

When Mack was a franchisor, he had signed to a strict condition stating that he could not open a property rentals business within a two-mile radius of his previous branch for a period of twenty-four months. I felt so stupid and annoyed at myself that I missed something as critical as that before the store was purchased.

Remember what I said earlier about owning a franchise. You will always be at the mercy of the franchise owner, even after you have quit.

We took the matter to a franchise specialist solicitor, who informed us that the legal action was valid and had been raised in the High Court of London.

This meant we needed a solicitor who was based in London to represent us; the cost of this was around £50,000 ($75,000).

We had both made another monumental and catastrophic slip up; we now had a store, purchased by Mack's parents, that couldn't be opened. To make matters worse, we had to pay loan payments on a store we were unable to open. This just added to the already mounting pile of expenses.

At this point, I had additional funds in Clear Investment that I could utilise as working capital, so I contacted Ameen with a view to requesting them.

Strangely, his phone was still off so I left another voicemail. Three days passed and he still had not returned my call. That same afternoon, one of my investors at Clear Investment called to say that their cheques had bounced. I thought it was some kind of prank. Then, another two investors called to say the same thing.

The last time I checked there was £360,000 ($530,000) in cash sitting in the account. Iftikhar and I went to the bank, only to find that the account was overdrawn. They explained that Ameen had cleaned the account dry. He had made payments to his personal account, written all sorts of cheques and made numerous payments to his mortgage accounts.

My heart sank and I felt sick to my stomach. This was our money; we'd worked so hard for it and in an instant, it was all gone.

Mack and I agreed we would not take any salary from Clear Lets until we made a profit.

The only income I had left was the rental income I was getting from my own properties, but it would not be enough to cover my household expenses.

At certain times in our lives, some of us will find ourselves broken. It takes true strength to pick up the pieces.

My head wasn't in the game; I had never encountered this type of betrayal, but I had to just make the best out of my situation.

To make matters worse, I never got any closure on the situation with Ameen. I wanted to know why he'd done it. Eventually, I sent him a long email. He responded a few months later, claiming that he knew nothing about it and tried to pin the blame on me and Iftikhar.

Once I read this, I let it go. I know that is not easy for a lot of people to do but my father had taught me better than to hold a grudge, even though Ameen had left me with nothing.

I had been raised to not let anger get the better of me. As hard as it was, I focused on ways to handle the situation with the investors who lost thousands. Once that was resolved, my priority was expanding Clear Lets to ensure that it provided me with an income.

I had already made many mistakes and no doubt I was going to make a lot more. What I didn't realise was, there were many more to come; more than I had ever imagined.

CHAPTER FORTY-FOUR

Catastrophic Failure

Mack and I were still working hard to build the business; we needed to break even so that we didn't have to keep supporting it financially. When it came to the Glasgow store, our hands were tied for another eleven months until Mack's contract with his previous franchisor expired.

We managed to find a retired builder named Wesley, who started the renovation work slowly. This worked out really well as we could just pay him small sums each time he completed a piece of work, without financially burdening ourselves.

The loan payment for this empty store totaled £13,200 ($20,900) over eleven months; this was nothing compared to what we would have spent on legal fees defending Mack's case.

My father once said: "If it wasn't for solicitors, we wouldn't need solicitors.'

I have learned that in any legal wrangle or litigation, the only people who benefit financially are the solicitors for each side.

My advice is to, do what you can to directly resolve a situation with the other party without getting solicitors involved.

Before you begin your journey, keep the end in mind.

Mack and I both travelled from Glasgow to Fife each day; to be honest, it was quite a trek but we both laughed so much in the car that we didn't mind the journey. After all, we had spent almost ten years working together before we became business partners, so we knew each other better than we knew ourselves.

We both knew what we were working towards; our aim was to save as much money as possible so that we could keep paying Wesley to finish the Glasgow store.

I was upset that we still were not making money, so I started paying close attention to where our money was going.

The biggest expenses were employee salaries and what we paid to the Inland Revenue.

On top of this, one of the conditions of our loan was to provide the bank with quarterly management accounts. We needed to hire accountants to produce these accounts.

At first, I didn't notice the expense because we didn't have that many properties on our books, although once we'd bought the Kingdom Letting portfolio, then that was a different story. Accountants charge for time and it was taking longer for them to complete their work.

If it weren't for all these added expenses, we would have actually been making a profit and quite a substantial one at that.

One thing to remember, if you are self-employed, it is likely your biggest expense as an employer will be to the Inland Revenue.

Mack and I arranged a meeting with the bank. We told them that the accountancy fees were crippling us financially and we didn't understand why we had to complete management accounts when we haven't missed a single loan payment. The bank just made their excuses and said it was part of the terms and conditions.

One other error we'd made was to only set up one limited company. This left us exposed to any debtor; this meant if we missed a payment with any creditor and if they subsequently decided to take legal action, they could petition for liquidation to close us down.

If you are intending to open more than one store, set up a separate limited company for each one. Not only that, set up a different limited company for each area of your business.

This will offer you a great deal of protection. It was something that I should have done, but as I was new to high street branches, I simply didn't have the experience. However, I never made that mistake again, so I hope, if this advice is applicable to you, that it is invaluable.

We were drawing in new customers and gaining momentum. I was still feeling stressed and anxiety kept me awake at night. Every day was now proving to be more difficult for me.

I was suffering, struggling to even buy food on some days and doing everything I could to cut my household costs.

Remember, if you receive your salary at the end of the month, but within a few days of paying your household bills have very little money left over, take a look at where your money is going and cut back.

We were forced to hire more staff to meet the demands of our growing client base, which wiped out any additional profit.

Winston Churchill once said: "If you are going through hell, keep going"

I had to look at the bigger picture; I knew that once the Glasgow store was open, we wouldn't need to fund the business for much longer.

Week by week, Mack and I used whatever money we had to buy materials; our first priority was to get timber to set up the framing for the walls and the floor. We knew where to get the materials cheaply and we negotiated hard for further discounts.

We had three months left to finish the store and the only things left to do were install air conditioning, buy office furniture and purchase computer equipment so we borrowed more money for these items from an asset finance company.

Asset finance is very risky and lenders will offer it, but will charge high rates of interest as the asset always depreciates. Before you sign on the dotted line, just ensure that you can cover the payments.

If I had the choice again, I certainly wouldn't undertake any asset finance.

To make matters worse, the finance company was paying these contractors directly before any work was carried out. This didn't help as the contractors just got the money and then we'd have to keep chasing them to finish the work. This wasted another three months and we were no further toward opening the store.

Meanwhile, back in Fife, the Kirkcaldy store was getting busier; yet the Dunfermline store was losing stock rapidly.

I arranged a meeting with Mary to find out why. The issue was that the employees of this store were providing a poor level of customer service.

The staff had annoyed many customers that they were leaving bad reviews on Google. One person had even created a Facebook hate page about the company.

I had to take legal action to get the page removed as some of the comments on it were slanderous. But the bigger issue was that I needed to discover why customers felt the way they did and had gone to such extreme lengths.

Never let another person's bad behaviour degrade your own.

I could have let this get to me and kicked up a stink with my employees but I didn't. Instead, I focused on the factors that had caused such poor feedback about the service they provided.

It turned out that they lacked customer service training and didn't know how to empathise with customers. I spent quite a bit of time training them. However, once people develop bad habits, they are not so easy to change.

I decided to give it another six months to see if there was any improvement. I kept a very close eye on the situation. However when you have a lot of things going on, keeping an eye on something can sometimes prove more difficult than you think.

When you juggle too many balls in the air, eventually you will drop a few.

Things were moving quickly regarding our Glasgow store opening; Mack and I had managed to get almost everything ready and just needed to find employees.

In the interim, Mack was negotiating a deal to buy out another letting agent; he thought he could use their portfolio to give us a good start.

Since we were still funding everything from our own pockets, I questioned how we would pay for this. He said we'd find a way, which is good entrepreneurism but not a practical response.

The real magic in being an entrepreneur is always in your enthusiasm. It is the difference between mediocrity and accomplishment.

We finally finished and before we opened, we decided to invite friends and family over to celebrate our opening. Looking back, it was the wrong thing to do.

Sometimes those amongst you, even those you call your friends, can actually be the ones who pray that you don't succeed. The hardest part is figuring out who these people are.

CHAPTER FORTY-FIVE

Making Adjustments

Mack had finally negotiated the purchase of a second letting agency, Guardian Property. He had structured the purchase of this portfolio in such a way that we wouldn't be able to earn an income from the portfolio, as that income would be used to pay off the purchase in installments. This was the perfect solution for us because we didn't need to borrow any additional money for the purchase; Mack's entrepreneurial spirit had paid off.

The issue arose when we sent out letters to the Guardian's customers, announcing that Clear Lets had taken over and they would have to pay additional management costs.

We certainly didn't increase the management fees; the only additional expense would be VAT (Value Added Tax), as our company was VAT registered and Guardian property wasn't.

The landlords wouldn't spend any money on the upkeep of their properties; they let their tenants live in slum conditions but wanted to make sure they received their monthly income without fail.

Being angry at the little things is easy, but being able to smile at the hardest things is extraordinary.

I could have let it get to me, but needed the income, so I made the best of a bad situation.

In addition to this, there was a banking crisis going on; banks all over the world were in major trouble and were asking their respective governments for bailouts. Countries were going bankrupt on an unprecedented scale; it was something I had never seen before.

The reason for all of this was simple. The bankers had gotten into too much debt by lending more money to people who simply couldn't afford to pay it back.

This became a massive problem for landlords who wanted to buy property to rent; they couldn't obtain money from the bank unless they were willing to pay huge deposits.

You might think this would be great for letting agents, but it wasn't the case; if the landlords cannot finance their properties, there are no new properties for rental.

This wasn't a good time to be in the property market.

I wasn't really concerned about the governing factors of what was going on around me; I just had to make sure we survived the credit crunch everyone was going through.

This was harder than I anticipated. The three stores had been established and it seemed that the journey ahead was only going to get tougher.

Mack was also going through a difficult time at home. He was having problems with his wife; they were still living with his parents and his wife wasn't comfortable with this. He had just had his first child and another was on the way, so between being a father and a husband, he had a lot going on in his personal life.

Mack's wife's unhappiness at their living situation had taken a toll on my friend and I had never seen him as miserable as he was now.

Your life partner will determine eighty-five percent of your success or failure in life.

My staff noticed a change in him as well. I had eighteen employees over the three stores, so I really needed his support.

One day we had a meeting so I went to collect Mack from his house; when he got into my car, I noticed that he had a bad black eye. I asked him what had happened, and he told me that the previous night, his wife had gotten into a massive argument with everyone at home and the police had been called.

Later I found out that his wife had gotten Mack's mother thrown into police custody by claiming she had assaulted her. This wasn't true as his mum was at an age where she couldn't assault anyone.

I think he was embarrassed about the whole situation and his parents told him that his family needed to find a place of their own.

Mack's personal issues caused him to lose focus; his attendance suffered dramatically.

If you give 100 percent of your focus to your business, it will take care of itself. Never let your personal issues affect your business.

Given that our stores were still not breaking even, and we were still investing our own money into them, this wasn't a good time to have to deal with domestic issues.

Our Dunfermline store was continually losing customers from the rental portfolio we'd purchased from Kingdom Letting, and the staff still hadn't learned how to treat customers. I simply couldn't afford for this store to lose any more money. So I had to consider the cost of keeping this store open against the amount of customers I was losing due to the staff.

When things don't add up, it's time to start subtracting.

The Kirkcaldy store was very large and we had a basement the size of the Dunfermline one that we could utilise. We decided to move the employees to Kirkcaldy and close Dunfermline.

This didn't go down well with the employees; they started complaining about the distance they would have to travel to work. I think they should have shown some gratitude for the fact that they still had a job.

To make their new commute easier, I offered them a company vehicle and told them that they could share the fuel costs. I don't know about you, but I don't think many employers would offer that.

When they started to moan about the cost of fuel, I bent over backwards for them and told them I would cover fifty percent of their fuel costs as well.

If you treat people right in your business, they will treat you right ninety percent of the time

Once the staff had relocated to the Kirkcaldy store, they were under Mary's watchful eye, so I had one less thing for me to worry about. In addition, we were saving money, as we were no longer paying a rental for a store and other related expenses.

But, just when you think that things have gotten better,. another problem comes along.

The bank sent us a letter stating that the interest rate for our loan had been increased and that we hadn't submitted our quarterly management accounts.

The accountants couldn't keep up with the growing workload and provide the accounts in a timely fashion, so we were in breach of our covenant with the bank. This allowed them to increase our loan payments.

In business, sometimes you have to fight through the bad days to earn the best days.

However, it seemed that I was still fighting through the bad; every time I felt we were taking a step in the right direction, I would hit another brick wall.

I looked to God and asked him why he was giving me all these problems; most likely because I was the only one who could solve them.

CHAPTER FORTY-SIX

Employees and Partners

Our expenditure kept growing. Mack and I used company vehicles due to the amount of travelling we were doing, and the cost to run these was high.

They were a necessity but it was my fault not taking a closer look at this expense.

When I look back, I realise there were many things I could have cut expenditure for, such as printers and copiers, mobile phones and fuel costs. I could have shopped around for the best electricity and gas prices due to being in a recession.

I presumed that after we'd closed a store we would get back on track financially, but I was wrong.

I'm not the type of person who likes to put anyone out of work. I had been there myself and I knew what it was like.

Sadly, I should have been stronger and let some employees go as these individuals were like dead wood; they were taking advantage of my good nature and not contributing anything to the success of the business.

For any business to succeed, the people you employ must share your vision and goals. However, you cannot forget that the buck still stops with you; the tough decision to let people go when they don't share your vision falls to you.

Ninety-seven percent of people who gave up on their dreams and goals end up working for the three percent who didn't. So don't let this be you!

It doesn't matter if your business fails; dust yourself off, pick yourself back up and start again.

Thomas Edison failed repeatedly. On being told that he'd failed over ten thousand times, his response was legendary: "I have not failed. I've just found ten thousand ways it won't work." And he kept going until he invented the light bulb.

Walt Disney was bankrupt eight times and had two nervous breakdowns. Now he brings joy to the world.

We had a viewings assistant, Kat, whose job was to show prospective tenants around a property; if they decided to proceed, she would obtain a deposit from them to secure the property and provide them with application forms. Kat was also one of our tenants; she came to work for me because I thought she would be good for the business. I went on gut instinct when employing her. One of the fatal errors I made, which proved to be very costly for me, was never doing background checks on her previous employers.

Kat led a lifestyle, which exceeded her income. I gave her an opportunity and I was very fair with her; I even provided her with a company car and covered her fuel costs.

To my detriment, Kat was stealing large sums of money. When a prospective tenant paid her the deposit to secure the property, she would pocket the money and tell the tenant that their application would take around four weeks to process. During that four-week window, she would do the same with many others; she'd use the money taken from the last person who paid to cover the first person who paid.

Remember trust can sometimes take years to build, seconds to break and only very rarely can it be repaired.

I trusted her and she had stolen £20,000 ($31,500) from us. This cost we had to cover from our own pocket in order to refund all the customers whose money was stolen.

Kat didn't even show her face, yet the week before she was caught stealing, she threw a lavish birthday bash using money she'd stolen from our already struggling business. I offered Kat the option of returning the money she'd stolen from us within a week; she never did, so I contacted the police and she was charged and prosecuted for theft.

So, always ensure you carry out thorough background checks on your employees.

This was another incident, which I had to take responsibility for, and it cost me severely. It would be easy for me to blame Kat for the theft, but as I said, the buck stops with me as I employed her in the first place without carrying out the proper checks.

It was bad enough that a few years before, Ameen had stolen every penny from the company bank account and left me in a financial mess; now another person did the same.

As a result, the atmosphere in our stores was quite sombre and almost everyone was in shock. Mack was still going through his own struggles with his wife, and had two children with a third on the way, so he had even less time to spend on the business.

To be successful, you have to have your heart in your business, and your business in your heart. Spending one or two days a week to just show your face will not quite cut it.

Mack's wife gave birth to their third child, a baby girl who was seriously ill at birth; his first priority was to be with his family.

As a result, he had to take almost three months off work. I covered for him as best as I could, even though it meant I was working almost twenty hours a day. It didn't bother me as I would do anything for him; we were very close. We'd known each other for almost twenty years, so it was the least I could do for him.

In the Glasgow store, some employees took advantage of the situation, one employee especially. When she arrived at work, the first thing she would do was to stand outside and have a cigarette. After that, she'd go for a coffee while catching up on Facebook.

In essence, I was paying people to browse their social media when they should have been doing their work.

I was very close to all of my staff, this woman in particular as we'd worked together for years; she'd worked for me at the rentals franchise. I trusted her implicitly, which is why I'd given her the opportunity to run the Glasgow store. I was heartbroken that she'd broken my trust and I dismissed her from employment without hesitating.

Later, she lodged a tribunal case against me for unfair dismissal due to racism; this was complete nonsense and the case was thrown out of court.

I kept in touch with Mack almost daily to keep him posted on what was going on; one thing we both did was back each other's decisions.

I decided that I wanted to sell and move on to other things. I was sick of it and I think managing it by myself had taken its toll on me both mentally and physically.

Once Mack's daughter was healthier, she returned home and he returned to work. We sat down to discuss selling the business.

Whenever you start a new business from scratch, have an exit strategy in place.

We were entrepreneurs and we had started from nothing; in three years, we'd built a reputable brand, which was well respected. It was something that anyone would want to buy.

CHAPTER FORTY-SEVEN

A New Concept

There were many big organisations that were snapping up rental agents in order to get a foothold in the market and we'd located one. If we did sell, we could have left with a small profit to split between the two of us. Not much after all of the work, pain and heartache, but it would have allowed us to leave with our heads held high.

Mack said he would speak to his wife before making a decision. I told him that I needed a break and borrowed some money from my sister to go on holiday. Mack promised that he would spend more time in the business during my time off and work harder to make sure it was a success.

I had known him for almost twenty years; I knew he wasn't going to just change overnight so I took his word for it. While I was away, I kept worrying about what was going on in my absence, but I made a point to focus on my time off. I was in Phuket, Thailand, one of the most beautiful places I had ever been to besides the Maldives, where the people were so humble; there was nothing they wouldn't do for you.

I did what I always used to do when I was a kid: I went around the markets to watch the traders selling their merchandise and started to browse around. I felt all excited, looking for a new ideas and concepts.

Eventually I found one. It was noodles, but in a proper Chinese style box, something I always used to see in the movies. In the UK, most people just stick food in foil containers.

The concept was a franchise and involved no cooking, but the food tasted amazing and I felt this could make money to turn our luck around. They had branches all over the world, including three in London. I wanted to take Mack there, to show him this new venture that I wanted to get involved in when I returned from my holiday.

Always be creative, take risks and live your passion, because that's what makes you an entrepreneur.

When I came back from my holiday, I felt so refreshed and energised that I had a renewed passion. I think my passion was being drained out of me throughout my time at Clear Lets. I wanted to add value to other people's lives based on my own experiences, so I signed up to become a business mentor with our local chamber of commerce. This gave me the opportunity to meet other business owners, teach them using my own experiences and also learn from them. I loved every minute of it because it gave my life a new purpose.

This eventually led to me speaking about my business journey at events, to an audience of other business owners; subsequently, I became an inspirational speaker.

Mack and I went to view the noodle bar concept in London, called Yam Yam to Go. We met the owner, who showed us everything regarding the food production and the set up of the franchise.

It all looked amazing; the concept was new and fresh and would suit Scotland well, so we decided to proceed. Our set up costs were high and we knew it was a risk, but we were very confident that it would be a success.

We still weren't breaking even at Clear Lets; my intuition presumed that we would do so within twenty-four months of trading. Now that we were approaching forty-eight months, I was becoming concerned.

Another factor was all the maintenance costs we had to pay for our landlords. The issue was, if their property had a problem, we would have to send a contractor to do the repair. We had to pay the contractor from our own pocket until we could recover the money from the rent we received for that property.

Some months our cash flow would be down by thousands, which meant we were short to pay our other costs. It was something that had to stop, but it was beyond our control. The bank was not pleased because the payments showed up as deficits in our quarterly management accounts.

We'd also now committed to Yam Yam to Go. This was another business we'd have to start in order to get a return on our investment.

We financed the franchise and set up costs to establish in a shopping mall in Kirkcaldy and it was doing amazingly well until our supply of food was suddenly cancelled.

When we asked our franchisor why, we were informed that there was a dispute in the brand ownership and the following week we received a court summons for infringement on using the Yam Yam to Go name.

Even though Mack and I stated that we had a franchise agreement in place, we were informed that it wasn't valid since it hadn't been agreed with the person who held the trademark and registration.

There is a saying that to every bad, there is a worse.

Mack and I had agreed that I would manage the noodle bar and he would manage Clear Lets, but that he would cover for me when I needed a day off and vice versa.

He had just purchased a new home with his wife and was in the process of moving, so this kept him absent from Clear Lets again. After the move, his wife took it upon herself to renovate the property to her liking.

I would get calls from the employees, and even Sandy our bookkeeper, asking me if Mack was coming in today. I told them that he should have already been there. He'd promised me that he would work full-time.

When I texted Mack to ask why he was not in the office, he would tell me that he had to run a few errands for his wife. The excuses piled up; one day, it was picking out new carpets, the next he had to buy a TV, then it was choosing new lights for their living room. It was just one excuse after another.

I was running out of excuses for Mack's absence. By now, I think our employees had all figured out that he had decided to distance himself and stay at home with his wife rather than focus on a business that needed his attention.

I was almost at breaking point due to all of the stress, and I told Mack this. We talked at length, as openly and frankly as we possibly could in private. He said that he'd had a tough year because he hadn't had a proper place to live with his children following his wife's fallout with his parents. He felt stressed because his daughter had been ill for so many months, had three children in quick succession, had moved house and was running Clear Lets. The addition of the noodle bar was contributing to his stress.

I said that I would support him as best I could.

We'd sacrificed everything over the past four years, such as our relationships with our respective families. We'd used our entire life's savings to fund the business and had gotten into debt with Mack's parents, who'd bailed us both out on many an occasion. But we had to ask ourselves, was it worth it?

Both of us had stopped feeling joy, and so far, what we'd just endured was a road full of disappointments, no matter which way we turned.

Mack said he needed a break and that when he returned he would focus on the business. I no longer believed him and still wanted to sell Clear Lets. While Mack was away, the bank found out about our new noodle bar venture and it wasn't long before we were hauled up in front of them to explain our financial position.

We gave the bank as much assurance as we could but they felt very exposed because of the banking crisis. We had now fallen behind with our payments and received a letter from them, detailing our loan breach and recalling their money.

This left no working capital and we would have been breaking the law if we'd continued trading.

Just because your business feels more like a burden than a dream, it doesn't mean you failed. It may just mean you're ready for your next act.

With a heavy heart, we proceeded to close Clear Lets and cease all trading with immediate effect.

There comes a time in everyone's life when they need to decide whether to keep going or call it a day.

CHAPTER FORTY-EIGHT

A Nervous Breakdown

I also had to factor in Yam Yam to Go, as our noodle bar had lost its food supplier. As we couldn't afford to pay another franchise fee, or source another location in order to relocate, we had to close it. Having two business closures within a matter of weeks made me feel like a failure.

Our primary focus was the final closure of all matters concerning the business.

However, much to my astonishment, the demise of Clear Lets was portrayed in a different light by the media. I made front-page headlines. The newspapers stated that I had closed leaving over eight hundred people out of pocket and running off with millions.

To say I was in shock was an understatement. I was the face of the company, not Mack, so the press portrayed me in the worst light. Some stories claimed that I ran away to Africa with everyone's money and that a massive police investigation had been launched to find me. This press situation was all new to me; I didn't go and explain myself as I thought it would all blow over. I also did not have any money to sue them for libel.

If the press had bothered to interview me, they would've uncovered the real story. However, they chose not to and the effect was malicious and slanderous.

People only ever whisper about your success, but they shout from the rooftops about your failures.

I explained the situation to the police and confirmed that I was in the process of returning property keys and files to our clients. We handed over files and finalised accounts so that we could bring final closure to all matters concerning Clear Lets.

We were unable to return funds for around twenty percent of our customers, yet the press didn't give up and they kept printing lies about me. They claimed that another letting agent in Dunfermline was being appointed by forensic accountants to find out where the stolen money had gone. No such accountants were ever appointed!

The police confirmed that they were closing the case since it was not a criminal matter. However, that didn't stop the press from completely vilifying me in the business world.

I became concerned and wondered where they were getting this false information from; it turned out it was from some of my former employees.

These were staff that had worked for me for years. I'd done my very best to keep them in a job, provided them with an income even when it meant I sacrificed my own, and this was how my loyalty was repaid. I can count the people who stayed loyal to me after the demise of my business on one hand. Alison, Shagufta, Saira, Angela and Carole. The rest just turned out to be poisonous snakes.

I sold almost every personal possession I had, including my clothes, my mobile phone, my iPad and my birthday presents just to cover the losses.

However, the press didn't see any of that because that wasn't a story that sold newspapers. They were mostly interested in the failure.

As a result of all that bad press, I couldn't even find a job because if anyone typed my name into a search engine, all that showed up in the search results were the lies that the press had written about me.

They ruined my reputation and my career in one swoop, and it seemed as though they took great pleasure in bringing me down.

If people are trying to bring you down, remember that it means you are above them.

It was getting me down quite badly. I would be petrified to set foot out of the house and my heart sank when I heard a knock at the door. I had no source of income at this point because the property market was at rock bottom. I struggled to sell some of my rental properties so that I could cover my debts. Even if I'd managed to sell some properties, the market had dropped so badly that I would have still owed the bank money; I wouldn't be able to withdraw some equity to help with my cash flow.

The bank repossessed my remaining properties.

Everything was crumbling down around me and I felt like the walls were closing in. I struggled to sleep and would have panic attacks in the middle of the night.

I couldn't even afford to pay my child support and as a result, my children had to move out of their home. They moved in with me whilst their mother went back home to Pakistan to stay with her parents until my financial situation improved.

We were all residing in my one-bedroom apartment, which wasn't far from being repossessed. They slept on the floor, which wasn't ideal as they were both adults, but we had a roof over our head and that was the main thing.

It's a shame the press didn't write about that; they made out that I was living in a mansion overseas. Throughout this horrible ordeal, my children were a tremendous support.

I was aware Mack was also going through a difficult time after the business ended.

However, I didn't expect him to collaborate with his wife and blame me for the failure.

One day, we met at his parent's house to discuss what had happened. Mack's wife became the mouthpiece; she thought that she knew it all and stated how she would have done things differently. If that really was the case, maybe she should have let him come to work, instead of sending him on errands

I couldn't believe the rubbish that was coming out of her mouth; it didn't bother me, but I was bothered that Mack, my friend of more than twenty years and business partner, just sat in a corner with his mouth shut.

All business has its ups and downs. His wife was only motivated by greed; if money had kept falling into her hands, then I'm sure she wouldn't have uttered a word against me.

She was happy to share the good times with him but not the bad.

Everyone wants happiness but no one wants the pain. However, you can't make a rainbow without a little rain.

Next, his wife accused me of stealing money from Clear Lets and transferring it into my own personal bank account.

She threatened to have her brothers "break my legs" if I didn't provide her with my personal bank statements.

Mack told me to just give her the statements to shut her up. I printed out my personal bank statements and took them to Mack's parent's house so that his wife could look over them. I made everything easy to read and explained any transactions in clear bold pen so that her small mind could understand.

Did I get an apology after I produced my bank statements? No.

Life becomes easier when you learn to accept an apology you'll never get.

What hurt me the most was that Mack let his wife accuse me of theft without saying a single word to defend me.

Sadly Mack and I had to keep in contact because his parents still owned the Glasgow store of Clear Lets and we had shared responsibility for the payments on the property.

This was not easy for me. I was in a position where I had no income, no savings and no job. To cover my share, my daughter Anah loaned me the money each month out of her student bursary; she covered my share of the loan payment until we got it sold.

I couldn't pay my own mortgage and I was in arrears with my mortgage lender. It wasn't long before the sheriff officers starting knocking on my door to serve their court summons for repossession.

I could barely sleep. If I did fall asleep, I would wake up having a panic or anxiety attack and breaking out in cold sweats. I wasn't eating either and lost a lot of weight. Putting even the smallest thing in my mouth would just make me physically sick.

One of the scariest realisations is that the only thing that you can save is yourself.

The slightest thing would make me worry in a major way. I would cry for hours and I kept asking myself the same question: 'What the hell is wrong with me? And why am I like this?'

Your greatest pains will become your greatest strengths.

I was deeply depressed but I couldn't figure out why. Was it because of the demise of my business? Or was it from the way the press had humiliated me with all their false allegations?

Maybe it was the shock of the employees, whom I'd kept in work for years on end, turning on me.

These employees had the audacity to take money from me for years; I bent over backwards accommodating them in every possible way, yet I got this treatment in return. Even to this day, Mary, Sandy and the sacked Dunfermline store manager write and post pathetic comments about me on their social media pages. Yet, to this day I have never said anything to them or drop to their vile level.

There were just so many factors running through my head, and each one was making me more and more stressed when I thought about it.

I'm a very private person. I didn't know who to speak to; the friends I thought I'd had turned out to be nothing more than acquaintances. My closest friend was Steven and although I entered his number into my phone several times, I just couldn't bring myself to dial. I didn't want him to hear or see me as broken as I was. I didn't want my sister Shabana to see me this way either because she was the one who knew how strong I was, after everything our family had been through.

People were talking about me, but it wasn't as difficult for me to deal with as it was for my children and my sister.

I was so broke that month after month I sold whatever possessions I had left in my home, just to make enough money to keep a roof above our head.

I had very little left at home to sell, so I sold my bed and just slept on the floor; it was no big deal because I wasn't sleeping anyway.

Your true strength is being able to hold it all together when everyone expects you to fall apart.

But I wasn't able to hold it together and if anything I was crumbling. I couldn't even speak to people without starting to cry, which was embarrassing.

Days would go by where I just sat on my bedroom floor feeling sorry for myself and asking continually how I'd ended up in this situation.

Once again, I was angry with God; I asked why he hated me so much and bet that he was laughing at me.

I was just looking for someone to blame other than myself, even though I took full responsibility for my actions.

I became really sick as a result of being so frail. I had lost almost three stone as I hadn't been eating due to stress.

My mind kept playing tricks on me and it felt like I had voices in my head. One was telling me to kill myself and end all the agony; the other was saying you are much stronger than that, you're not a coward who would take the easy way out and leave your children without a father.

You can be miserable or motivate yourself. Whatever it is that has to be done, it's always your choice.

CHAPTER FORTY-NINE

Getting Back Up Again

I finally needed to motivate myself to pick up the phone and call someone for help, but I just couldn't do it. I didn't want to burden anyone with my problems.

My children were fantastic; they were too young to remember what I went through when they were babies but as young adults, they shared my pain. This gave me the strength to live out another day. I had made many mistakes in my life, but my children were not mistakes.

Nine months passed and I still hadn't talked to anyone about it; I think that is what made the situation worse.

One thing I have learned is that there is no need to suffer in silence, and there is no shame in seeking help.

Finally, I managed to speak to Steven about my situation, and we spent almost five hours talking on the phone; a fairly normal amount of time for us anyway.

He was in shock and asked me why I hadn't called him earlier. We could have worked this out; I explained that I didn't want to burden him with my problems.

Steven told me that there was no shame in what I was going through. I thought that was silly, and that this was only a bad phase in my life which would pass with time, but the more I thought about it, the more I realised he was right.

I told him that the horrible portrayals of me in the press, and Mack's betrayal, had really got to me.

Difficulties in life don't happen in order to destroy you, but to help you realise your true hidden potential.

My nervous breakdown was a result of losing Mack from my life.

I'd shared something special with him for over twenty years. We'd become business partners; we'd travelled the world together on numerous holidays and had such laughter together. We'd watched our children grow, shared in each other's pain and joy. He was a big part of my life, and it felt like I had lost a brother.

Your happiness in life is dependent on the quality of your thoughts.

Steven made it very clear that I was wrong to feel so heart-broken over the loss of him. He told me that Mack had chosen his path, and I needed to let him go and move on with my life.

This wouldn't be easy, so I needed to get help.

I went to see my doctor. Sometimes your doctor is the only person you can trust to not be judgemental. My doctor was also a good friend, so I asked him for an "off record" conversation. I explained everything to him, detailing all I had been through over the past year; the panic attacks, being unable to eat, being sick all the time, the suicidal tendencies, and the constant crying and emotional rollercoaster I endured every day.

He confirmed that I was going through a nervous breakdown. He told me that he could prescribe anti-depressants to help get me through it, but this would be placed on my medical record.

My doctor knew I hated any sort of pills; even if I have a headache, I won't take a painkiller, let alone anti-depressants.

I just needed someone to talk to; someone who was in the same situation as me, so he said he would look for local groups who conduct sessions in my area. I could attend these groups anonymously without anything going on my medical record.

True to his word, he called me the very next day with details, and I arranged an appointment with the support groups and started attending. It was great; there were people there with different problems, but everyone felt relieved after sharing their feelings. Even though I am a private person, I opened up and poured my heart out to complete strangers. The weirdest thing was that these people didn't judge others, and they offered me more support than my so-called friends who had abandoned me.

When you fall upon hard times, the one luxury is that it will always reveal your true friends.

Steven called me almost every day to check up on me; that's what friends do. I think he was scared that I would do something stupid like harm myself. He mentioned that he had found a lady who was a mind healer; maybe she could help me.

Her name was Asha and, if I'm being honest, I didn't know what to make of her at first. She seemed a little odd;

however, my father had taught me not to judge so I kept an open mind. She sat me down on a chair while she sat on the floor in front of me, and asked me why I was here. I replied that I honestly didn't know. Asha told me to close my eyes so that she could ask the question again: "Why are you here, Tahar?"

I remember the exact words that came out of my mouth. I said it was because I felt broken, dejected, and also lost and lonely. Her reply was so warm; she said: "let's heal all of your pain."

Failures are part of life. If you don't fail, you don't learn. If you don't learn, you can never change.

Asha told me that I had an amazing opportunity in front of me; the opportunity to rebuild my life in a better way than before, and mould myself into the man I really wanted to be. My life must have a purpose, as without purpose, we are just empty vessels travelling in a body and passing time.

Her advice was to stop being bitter about everything that had happened, and to start being thankful for it; to look at it as a blessing.

I found this a little difficult at first. I was about to be evicted.

Remember, if you don't control your attitude, it will end up controlling you.

In a way, Asha was right. When she asked what I was doing with my time, I said nothing; I couldn't focus on anything because of the way I was feeling.

Asha advised me to learn new skills and create a new mind-set, as I had a wonderful opportunity. I could be a gift to millions of people around the world.

Creating a new mindset was new to me and I didn't even know where to start. I couldn't even think about doing it, what with everything else going on around me.

Life has many ways of testing your will. Either nothing happens or everything happens all at once.

Asha explained that I had two options; I could either make progress or make excuses.

She told me to read and follow Deepak Chopra. Asha said that he was a wellbeing expert who would help me to heal from the inside out. I would have done anything to end the pain and torment I was going through; if it meant following Deepak Chopra, then so be it.

The man was actually amazing, and he opened up my mind to all of the infinite possibilities I had the potential to achieve.

A month or so later, I lost my home, but my only concern was my children. They had saved enough money to get a place of their own, with their mother, who had returned from Pakistan. I chose to see the positive in this, rather than the negative. I realised that whatever had happened over this past year, I had to be thankful for where it brought me.

Being homeless once again was no big deal this time, and I was glad it was all over. No more worrying about people knocking on my door, or what new debt notice I would be served with next.

The bank decided to sequestrate me and declared me bankrupt, which was another blessing as it stopped the press printing false stories about me.

Asha was a great influence in my life, and encouraged me to read and follow people who had been on similar journeys to mine, such as Les Brown, Brian Tracy, Jack Canfield, and Dr. Wayne Dyer. These were all people I had never even heard before.

This led to me looking up other people, like Oprah Winfrey, Will Smith, Barbara De Angelis, and Marianne Williamson, who never gave up on life.

I surrounded myself with these people's books, YouTube videos, blogs, tweets, and Facebook posts because the messages were all positive, all inspirational, and from the heart.

Surround yourself with people who make you better, who help you to grow, and who love and celebrate life. I believe that you will soon be a product of your surroundings.

Even though I had no roof over my head and no money, for the first time in my life I wasn't even worried, and felt no stress.

I'm not saying that everything in my life was perfect, far from it. I still felt sick and I had panic attacks, but less frequently.

My situation had distanced me from my friends. Iftikhar often called or emailed to see how I was, but I never answered his calls. When I saw his number come up on my phone, I would just start to cry hysterically.

I was ashamed and I didn't want Iftikhar to know what I was really going through. He had always seen me as a strong, emotionally intelligent individual, who let nothing faze him. He was also a very busy man and I didn't want to burden him with my woes. For now, as long as I had Steven, my children, and my sister Shabana around me, that was all I needed.

What lies behind us and what lies before us are tiny matters compared to what lies within us.

In order to get myself back on track, I had to put a structure in place. Every morning, I would go for a walk in the local park whilst listening to Les Brown on my headphones. This man wanted to make a difference in the world and he was a massive inspiration to me. His motivational tapes were being implanted into my brain. I did the same thing every day; I listened to various people whilst on my walk around the park.

By the way, Will Smith is amazing. I only knew of him as an actor, not as an actual person. He has such an amazing, positive attitude, the like of which I'd never witnessed in my life. In one video, he said that if you intended to run against him on a treadmill, he wouldn't stop until he died on it.

It is in our failures that we discover our true desire for success.

In the afternoon, I would set aside time to read books. One author I enjoyed was Brian Tracy, who just seemed to know everything about life. I read his book Maximum Achievement, writing it all down as I read it so that it implanted in my head. Dr Wayne Dyer and Marianne Williamson were a little like Deepak Chopra, because they promoted inner-peace.

In three months, I couldn't believe how much I was reading, writing, and listening to; I was feeling better every day.

What you do today can improve all of your tomorrows.

The one thing I realised through all of this was that in my life, I had surrounded myself with the wrong people. I needed to be around people who shared my vision, people who didn't belittle my ambitions.

Be thankful for the difficult people in your life. They will show you exactly who you don't want to be.

Falling down is how we grow, but staying down is how we die. I was rising, albeit slowly, but I was becoming stronger with each passing day. I never begged anyone for things I had the power to achieve myself.

Sometimes, being pushed to the wall gives you the necessary momentum to get over it. I felt I was getting closer and closer to that.

I hadn't met very many people whilst going through my nervous breakdown; I just didn't have the confidence to speak to people any more. I felt like I couldn't trust anyone, after the way the majority of my former employees had turned on me.

Even though I was broke and homeless, I wanted to help other people less fortunate than me. I started volunteering at a homeless shelter's soup kitchen, and loved it. The time I spent there gave me a sense of purpose because I was doing something for others.

Seeing people's smiles as I served them food was priceless; for once in my life it felt amazing to give, even though I could only give my time. So I gave with all my heart.

I kept in mind what Asha had said to me about needing to find a purpose in life. One day, as I was walking in the park listening to Les Brown, it came into my head. I should use my voice to bring a message to anyone suffering the same difficulties I had gone through.

Sometimes God takes away everything you thought you wanted in order to bring you everything you've ever dreamed of.

Instead of being bitter about losing everything, I became happy. I lost it all; it was all materialistic, and served no purpose other than to facilitate a certain lifestyle.

It didn't fill the void that was missing in my life; I wanted to be a giver, and help others to achieve their goals. If none of this had happened to me, I wouldn't have been able to write this book. Instead, I would still be managing a business and dealing with all of the associated stress.

The whole experience taught me something: what to value; who my friends were; and it renewed my faith in God. Now I realised that this entire struggle had happened for a reason.

Remember that the bigger the struggle you face, the bigger your destiny will be.

Everything that happened had changed me as a person. I learned humility and my attitude changed to be more gratuitous.

I compiled a list of everything I was grateful for in my life and read it every night before I went to sleep. The list gave me a sense of purpose, reminding me that I wanted to live my life serving others.

Hardships often prepare ordinary people for extraordinary destinies. For the first time in eighteen months, I really believed that this was the case, and I was wearing something that I hadn't worn in a very long time: a smile.

I kept busy reading books, and writing about what I was learning so that I could continually refresh my memory.

Negative talk produces negative thoughts. Negative thoughts produce negative results.

My life had no room for negativity now. Positive people surrounded me, through the books I read, and I knew that these were the type of people I needed in my life.

I didn't need reminding of where I had been or where I was. I focused only on where I actually wanted to be. I wanted to give others inspiration and motivation so that they could succeed no matter what challenges they might be facing.

Some people are put on this earth to make a difference in other people's lives; this was my opportunity to make a difference.

Life is a chance, so take it. The person who goes furthest is the one who is willing to do and dare.

CHAPTER FIFTY

Inspirational Speaking

I joined a local speaking club called Toastmasters, where I met some incredible people. I was completely honest with everyone about the fact I was going through a nervous breakdown, and working my way back from it. No one judged me; if anything, they supported me immensely and became good friends.

By attending the speaking club, I had found my voice again and my confidence grew simply because of the people around me. I'd always wanted to be the best at whatever I did, and speaking was no different. After speaking on different topics, everyone would fill out feedback forms about my speaking, so that I could improve.

Over the months, I had changed into a completely different person. Gone was the old Tahar. During the previous two years, I felt like I had aged twenty years, and now I had more grey hairs and a few more wrinkles.

But the one thing that had returned was my smile.

One day, whilst on my road to recovery, I was browsing the internet and saw a picture of a man named Joel Osteen. I didn't know who this man was, but one thing that

I liked was his warm smile. So I clicked on his website and found that he was a pastor at Lakewood Church in Houston, Texas, and that he was married to a lovely lady. On his website, he had videos of his previous messages and I decided to click on one of them. I was amazed at this man's positive attitude towards life. He was so motivational and inspirational through the messages that he preached.

It is during our darkest moments that we must focus, in order to see the light.

Joel was a man who had "unconditional love," something I'd never experienced before. The more I watched him, the more I learned to "love unconditionally" the people around me, and life itself. This man wanted to give back to others; call it a message from God. It was light to people who may have been going through adversity, and to me, he was a blessing.

We all need people in our lives that can guide us when we hit a crossroads, and most of us will look towards our parents, but I didn't have that luxury. My relationship with my own children changed thanks to Joel Osteen. I learned how to be a better father, and how to teach them to learn from my journey. They started saving money rather than wasting it so they could have a better future. I taught my children how to be givers, not takers, and how to be grateful for everything they have no matter how small it may seem. So I owe a massive thank you to Joel Osteen for making such a difference to my life.

Motivational speakers can only guide you in the right direction; it's your own thought process that can change the way you think about things.

If motivational speakers get you through the hard times, and you come out the other side, be thankful that they were placed in your life for a reason, somehow. Through these individuals, I had learned to embrace my struggles as I wasn't where I was always going to be.

Strong people stand up for themselves. Stronger people stand up for others.

Finally, I realised I was ready to take on the world again, only this time, I was much stronger, both mentality and physically.

CHAPTER FIFTY-ONE

Better and Stronger

Coming back from any sort of adversity is never easy. I could have chosen to wallow in self-pity but it would have served no purpose. I just needed to surround myself with the right people, who would support me through the dark days and help me get out of the hole I was in.

Whatever consumes your mind controls your life. The only thing that I had to do now was to not look back, and use my pain as fuel to remind me of my own inner strength.

I wanted to get back on track, but this time I wanted to start an internet business. The reason for this was simple; it would mean no overhead costs, no worrying about high street premises, or about staff betraying me.

While I had been engrossed in reading, I'd also studied how to build and market websites. I'd learnt about search engine optimisation, and how to build Facebook business pages, Twitter, Google+ and other social media pages.

Not only did I know how to build a website, I also knew how to design one, so instead of searching for ridiculous, overpriced Internet companies, I decided that I would bring in people that wanted my custom on my budget.

I found a website called *People Per Hour*, and what a genius idea. You can hire anyone you want in almost every field, who can get the work done for you.

I posted a job request (it's free) and gave a short description of what I required. Within a few hours, almost fifty people had replied.

So instead of thinking outside the box, get rid of the box.

I wanted to get into the weight loss industry; rising levels of obesity worldwide meant that the market would never die out; it would sustain itself in the long term.

Next, I had to find a wholesaler for my products; I found one in the USA who would design my own brand and labels, and then send the products to me. I needed guaranteed quality, and their manufacturing process was under strict FDA guidelines. I've never wanted to sell a poor product to a customer; I have always believed that a person should never sell anything that he wouldn't buy himself. So much so, I used my sister, Shabana, as a test subject for the weight loss products.

After one month, my sister lost over two stone, so at least the product worked. All I had to do now was market the products.

Facebook was a medium used primarily by small companies, as a way of marketing their products to consumers. I had learned everything there was to know about their promotional opportunities, and how to get a page set up on Facebook very quickly. Not only that, I learned how to do very specific, targeted marketing to reach the customers I needed. This meant that I didn't waste money on adverts like I had done in the past.

I borrowed some money from my daughter Anah. Over the next three months, I learned how to build a Facebook audience and get a massive following for my products.

I decided to start with a very small budget to bring new consumers to my business page. It wasn't a lot, but it was all I could afford with the money I had.

In life, take a chance. You never know how absolutely perfect something could turn out to be.

I wasn't one to carry my past around with me; I decided to place it under my feet and use the experiences as stepping stones to rise upward.

Remember, you are not giving up. You are just starting over.

I didn't need to buy stock because the wholesaler that I had used to source my products would provide a drop-ship service for my customers. I lost around twenty percent of the profit from each sale, but it also meant I didn't have to buy stock in bulk and have it sitting around, gathering dust, because I hadn't made a sale.

Success is never achieved through the size of our brain; it is always achieved through the quality of our thoughts.

My only expenses were setting up a website and the budget for Facebook advertising.

This still left me with a little money to get some SEO work carried out on my website. Again, rather than waste thousands on large-scale organisations, I hired freelancers at a fraction of the cost.

As I said earlier in my book, I promised to explain how anyone could start a business with a small outlay.

The first month my website went live, I had around one thousand Facebook fans, and I sold thousands of pounds worth of produce, creating a decent profit. This was amazing; I had covered my investment and repaid my daughter.

CHAPTER FIFTY-TWO

A Different Approach

Within a month, my business was debt free, something I hadn't managed during the four years that I had owned Clear Lets. I was posting on Facebook at least seven times a day to engage with my followers; the difference was I wasn't just posting adverts on sales. I was engaging with my followers and having conversations about my products. As my fan base grew, so did my sales, and what was even more amazing was that my products worked and I got repeat customers.

Three months later, I had six thousand fans on my Facebook page, and a huge customer base that I had created from nothing. Sales were almost doubling every month as was my net profit. I didn't spend any of it. Instead, I invested it all back into buying stock in bulk; this allowed me to increase my profit margins as I was no longer losing twenty percent to my supplier who shipped the products.

Obviously, this meant a lot more work for me because I had to package my products and ship them to my customers. However, I contacted Royal Mail, the UK's postal service, and opened an account because I was sending out products in volume. I negotiated my rates, which meant I could earn additional money from what I saved in postage costs.

In a little under a year, I had almost twenty thousand Facebook fans who were repeat customers, so I decided to start selling my products on eBay and Amazon.

Fear and faith have something in common. They both ask us to believe in something we cannot see.

Opening an eBay store was easy, and as I had done this before it took me less than a day. However, opening one with Amazon wasn't so easy. I hired a freelancer to do it, which saved me a whole lot of time.

Remember that your time is money, so learn how to value it. A freelancer allows you to do other things and saves you hours of time wasted. So learn how to value your time; if you want to succeed in business, this is highly important.

CHAPTER FIFTY-THREE

Hard Times Don't Last Forever

I had established an online business, and was working for almost twenty hours a day. I wasn't earning millions, but it was my own hard-earned money. It was enough for me to get a place of my own. I could work from home, run a small car, and even buy a few essentials.

Hard times may have held you down, but they won't last forever.

The difference is that I learned to be extremely prudent with my money. I started to watch my spending, and worked out whether I needed each item, based on its value.

I did this with everyday items; just by shopping conservatively and choosing the best offers, I saved hundreds of pounds a month. I could effectively start another two businesses with what I saved. So take my advice and watch every penny you spend, or use the app at the *Expensify* website to better manage your money. It will help you to keep a track of all your unnecessary expenditure.

I had disciplined myself with money, more than I had ever before. I lived on 50 percent of my income, and I would use this money to pay for my rent, car, bills, and living expenses. The remaining 50 percent, I split into 10 percent segments.

50 percent - Living Expenses

10 percent - Money to be invested into Stocks and Shares and never touched

10 percent - Money deposited to savings – rainy day money, so to speak

10 percent - Money I spent on myself as a treat; the mind needs this or else saving money isn't fun

10 percent - Money donated to charity

10 percent - Money I spent to buy books, go to training seminars, and on other avenues to increase my knowledge.

The last two years I had been broke and homeless. My car had been repossessed, on my birthday of all days, and I never wanted to be in that situation again.

Learning to live this way is hard, but if you never want to be broke again, it has to be done.

Repeat these words after me: "**I will never be broke again.**" Repeat this daily for twenty-one days.

Concentrate on your work rather than your worries. If you don't fight for what you want, don't cry for what you've lost.

I became an extremely humble person. I showed so much humility that everywhere I went, people would notice. They would always comment that I was a lovely person and tell me that it was a pleasure to have met me.

To be honest, I can't recall very many people who'd said that before, or maybe I just hadn't noticed. However, now my attitude was to be grateful. I began wishing on others what I wanted for myself.

Your outer world is a mirror of your inner world. Wherever you look, you'll see yourself as everything reflects back to you.

For the first time, I loved my life thanks to the grace of God; I finally felt as though I served a purpose.

My father always used to tell me: "The real measure of your wealth is how much you would be worth if you lost all your money. No one has ever become poor by giving"

I finally understood this sentiment.

As my Internet venture was providing me with an income, I started to distribute around ten percent of my profit to charity. The causes closest to me were homelessness and drug addiction, as I have been homeless twice and had a sister with drug problems.

I learned one thing whilst supporting these two causes. **Never look down on people unless you are helping them up.**

My life became all about helping others. I started to volunteer as a mentor, helping young people to start their own businesses. I supported them through the start-up process and put them in touch with good freelancers that could help their ideas come to life.

As this was something I was very passionate about, I set up a new business called Social Media Management and Consulting. I created this company to help entrepreneurs start up their own businesses at a nominal cost. If an entrepreneur can't afford the outlay, I fund their website start-up costs in return for a small equity stake. Once they make money, they buy my equity stake back at the value of investment, with no interest or profit for me.

This might seem like a lot of work to get no money in return, but I provided additional services to support them, which created income. It allows these young entrepreneurs to be who they want to be and achieve financial independence without sacrificing their dignity.

Life seemed to be providing for me, and not in the financial sense. I was giving something to the universe, so it was giving something back to me. I loved every moment of it.

One day, out of the blue, Iftikhar called me. I hadn't had the courage to talk to him before, but I finally answered his call and he asked if I was free to meet up for a coffee and a chat.

Friendship is not about whom you have known the longest. It's about who walked into your life, said I'm here for you, and proved it.

We hugged when we saw one another; it had been almost two years since we'd seen each other. He commented on how much weight I had lost and said it was good to see me smiling again.

Iftikhar informed me that the property market was thriving in London and he'd been there for most of the past year, building some contacts to break into the market place.

At no point did Iftikhar discuss the fact that my relationship with Mack had ended, which was kind of him. I had put it all behind me and I had no need to open old wounds.

I regret nothing in my life, even though my past was full of hurt, simply because it all made me who I am today.

Remember, you don't need a certain number of friends, just a number of friends you can be certain of.

He asked if I'd be interested in working together again, in London, building a network so that we could conduct property sales as we'd done before. I said I would need to think about it and get back to him in a few days.

I'd never dealt with the London market before, but I was willing to give it a go.

If you fight hard, know who you are, and are proud of who you are, you will always have a good chance of winning.

I wanted to ensure that I had a sales force that could sell projects for us, without the headache of having actual employees. I vowed that I would never hire employees again.

In London, there are over one thousand six hundred real estate agents all fighting for business; I just had to find an angle that would get them all calling me, rather than me contacting them directly.

I met with Iftikhar again and asked how he would like to structure the business. As I was working in partnership again, I wanted to ensure our job roles were clearly defined so that we both knew our responsibilities.

If you are getting into a business with a partner, ensure that you get a proper legal partnership agreement drafted that clearly outlines your job roles.

This saves the hassle of dealing with these issues later on if things don't work out with your partner.

Iftikhar told me that if I could get him a meeting with potential investors, he could explain how our package worked and get them to work with us.

So this was my remit. In the UK, most real estate agents use a portal to advertise their properties, for example Right-move or Zoopla. A person can also send bulk email enquiries to agents through these portals. You are better off doing this in case your email ends up in the spam folder, and being dealt with by the admin assistant rather than the decision makers.

A little lesson for you there; if you are contacting businesses directly, follow the link to their company website so that your email penetration rate is at a hundred percent.

My next task was getting these real estate agents to contact me. I had to write something in my enquiry that I knew would capture their interest.

If you don't believe you can do it, you will never find the motivation necessary to start. If I'm being honest, it wasn't that difficult since we had almost thirty properties to sell. Almost any estate agent would bite your hand off in order to sell your projects at this volume.

In my email to the real estate agents, I said I that had thirty properties for sale and rental in their area, and asked if a director could call me to discuss this opportunity. I only sent this message to ten agents in case I was bombarded with more calls than I could handle. The response was phenomenal. All of them called me back within hours of receiving my email enquiry. The projects we sold came with a guaranteed rental for twelve months, which was paid as a lump sum in advance. They included full interior design and furniture packages, plus service charges and ground rent paid for twelve months, with a contribution towards legal fees as well.

To attract positive things in life, start by giving off positive energy.

Our package was no different to what it was before, but now we were selling property in London instead of Scotland. Property values in London start at around one million whereas in Scotland, they start at around one hundred thousand. We would have to sell ten properties in Scotland for every one sold in London to get the same level of sales commission.

Selling one property is far easier than selling ten properties but this time, I didn't need to find investors directly. I was already tapping into the client banks these real estate agents had built up over the years.

The added bonus was that I only needed to pay these agents if they sold a property, unlike having to pay an employee every month whether they sold or not. I had learned from all of my past and ensured that I had no unnecessary expenses.

Sometimes a poor past turns out to be the best investment in a promising future.

Once I discussed our product with these agents, I arranged for Iftikhar to meet with them for a coffee and a chat.

CHAPTER FIFTY-FOUR

Reaping Rewards for my Hard Work

I moved to London and I had introduced Iftikhar to over five hundred agents in a year; this became our sales force. If the agents didn't sell anything, it was more of a loss for them than it was for us.

All of a sudden, I realised that in just under a year I had built up a massive network of people, from scratch, in a completely new city. Not only that, we were also selling projects now totaling billions instead of millions.

This also meant our profit was one hundred times the value it had been in Scotland, a far cry from a few years back, when I was broke, homeless, and having a nervous breakdown.

I finally realised I was back at full strength mentally, physically and financially, and far more successful than I had ever been in my life.

I handed over my online weight loss business to my daughter, Anah; she could manage it full-time because she had just graduated from university with full honours. I felt so proud to be her father. My oldest son had also found work after university; I was proud that he had kept his head down, listened to his father and hadn't followed in my footsteps.

I loved being in London, I felt as though I was a completely different person there. It felt like a new start with new friends in a city that never slept. Everyone was hungry for success, and people didn't have time to moan and whine about how bad their lives were like they did elsewhere. Iftikhar and I met with motivated, desirous people on a daily basis, and their attitudes were infectious.

What hurts you today makes you stronger tomorrow. The moment you feel like giving up, remember the reason you held on for so long. You can't start the next chapter of your life if you keep re-reading the last one. I realised I was spending time with people who made me happy, not people I had to impress. In order for me to become successful, the old me had to die and give birth to the man who I was always meant to become.

Don't let yourself get sidetracked by people who are not on the same track as you, and never regret your past. Only regret any time you have wasted with the wrong people.

The only person you are destined to become is the person you decide to be.

I decided what I wanted to be, and what I wanted to do with my life. I wanted to be an inspirational speaker and share my journey.

My goal is to provide a hundred thousand people with funds, to start their own businesses. For me, this would mean helping a hundred thousand dreams come true, so that those people could add value to others as well. I wanted to devote more of my time to charitable causes, to help others who were less fortunate using the profits generated by my business.

The people who endure the biggest struggles in life are often the ones whose hearts shine the brightest.

I had faced the greatest challenge I could ever face, and discovered who I was in the meantime. I was content with where I had been, and, finally, I was proud of who I was.

For me, it was all about creating a life that felt good on the inside, not one that just looks good on the outside. I wasn't afraid to dream bigger.

I also realised that the only people that I needed in my life were the ones who showed me that they needed me in theirs. I also realised that the years that I'd struggled were the most beautiful of all, because they taught me that the meaning of my life was to find my own special gift.

CHAPTER FIFTY-FIVE

Finding Peace and Continuing to Grow

Iftikhar and I are still business partners to this day, and we own a very successful property investment company that now operates globally. He stuck by me and got me back on my feet, bigger and better than before, and asked for nothing in return. Iftikhar's life has always been about giving; this was one of the biggest lessons that I learned during the darkest days of my life.

Instead of hiring employees, we employ freelancers, because if they don't perform, they are gone within twenty-four hours. We don't have to go through the bureaucracy of following formal disciplinary procedures, and waste money paying employees. We don't have to worry about industrial tribunals either.

I now conduct my trading through separate offshore entities, to ensure that I'm never embroiled in any legal issues again. Mistakes are often the beginning of any great enterprise so don't be afraid of making them; you will give birth to more in your future than you have lost in your past.

The path that I have now chosen contributes towards my growth, which means I feel at peace with others and myself.

To be older and wiser, you first have to be young and stupid and realise that everyone you meet has something to teach you.

You will never make yourself great by revealing how small someone else is.

Learn to give without remembering, and always receive without forgetting. We have all been put on this earth to discover our own path, and we will never be happy if we live out someone else's idea of life.

Enjoy the little things because one day you will look back and realise that they were the biggest things in your life. It is easy to join the crowd, but it is difficult to stand-alone.

I now have the privilege and honour of speaking to people across the globe; I speak to people who want to succeed in every aspect of their life. I have the privilege of speaking in schools, colleges, universities, and large corporations about my entrepreneurial journey.

If you wait until you are ready, you will be waiting for the rest of your life.

I decided to follow my dreams, otherwise I would have spent the rest of my life working for someone who did.

I love to serve others, and I realised, through my struggles, what the meaning of my life was.

My goal is to bring out the best in people and let them know they shouldn't be afraid, and not to give up on their dreams.

People without vision, hope, dreams, ambitions, or desire to win, will go out of their way to kill yours.

So take a chance and try to get what you want in life and don't watch your chance pass by. Don't worry about failure because every failure brings you a step closer to success.

CHAPTER FIFTY-SIX

You Were Born to Succeed

The things you want are always possible, but you might not have the knowledge to get them. Some people don't realise that the only real obstacle to fulfilling your dreams and goals is you.

The first thing you need to do is to choose a goal that is important to you, one that will make you a better person and help you grow. Tell yourself every day that things are going to get better for you, in every way. Become inspired by your own words. Every day is going to be a new day, so I suggest that you stop worrying about the past, because it doesn't matter anymore.

When you think that everything going wrong in your life is someone else's fault, you will suffer a lot. Whatever you are seeking in life, it is also seeking you. You must understand that deep within your heart if you are to attract the life you want.

Life is all about the law of attraction. If you have not already read the book or watched the film, "The Secret" by Rhonda Byrne, I suggest very strongly that you buy it and learn about how the law of attraction works in your life.

Clear your mind of the negative word "Can't" and immerse yourself in transforming yourself into whom you want to be.

In the process of discovering yourself, you will meet a lot of hardships that will challenge your resolve. So don't be afraid of stepping outside of your comfort zone, as believing in yourself is ninety-five percent of the battle. Only then can you live your best life.

We sometimes forget the obstacles were placed there to help you face life and become the person you were meant to be.

If you have a setback, it is just preparing you for a comeback.

The best way to move forward is to let go of the negative people in your life in relation to your dreams, and to only associate yourself with quality individuals. Don't run around with losers. Winners compare their achievements against their goals, while losers compare their achievements to those of other people.

The losers can't grow because they're too busy telling everyone else what their shortcomings are. Don't let these people break your spirit; shut them out of your world and focus on taking care of you.

Your success and failure is down to your relationships. Even if you failed at something, it doesn't make you a failure. That's what you did, not who you are.

Do your best not to make someone your priority if that person has made you an option. We're all going through something, but the trick is to go through it anyway. Success will not just come to you. You will need to seek it out, and do so with love and passion.

Every person comes into your life as a blessing or a lesson. Steven, Iftikhar, my children, and my sister Shabana were there for me during my darkest days. They were the biggest blessings of all because they were the ones who didn't just abandon me when I needed them most.

Are you in a relationship that is making you so angry, you feel that instead of living together, you are dying together?

The more positive your relationship, the more opportunities you will have to create a richer life, rather than putting on a mask and pretending that everything is fine.

Somewhere within you is a purpose, and it is through purpose that you will achieve your goals and dreams.

You were put on this planet for a reason, and if you believe in that, your blessings will increase as long as you take the time to appreciate them.

Look at your dreams and goals.

Are you chasing them or watching TV instead? Do you get up earlier every day to learn new things and improve yourself?

People that relentlessly pursue their goals get up every day and make a commitment to doing whatever is necessary to achieve.

People might tell you that you dream too big. I suggest that you reply by saying 'you think too small.' People may have said negative things about you in the past, but the good news is, these negative people don't determine your destiny.

Not everyone will understand your journey, and that's fine! It's not their journey to make sense of; it's yours, so stop putting yourself at the back of the line, and move forward at every opportunity.

Your life is a gift from God, and what you do with your life is your gift back to God.

Many of us are not living our dreams because we are living our fears. FEAR can stand for "Face Everything and Rise" or "Forget Everything and Run," the choice is yours!

Your biggest achievements will come from your biggest mistakes. No one can travel back in time to fix mistakes, but you can learn from them and forgive yourself for not knowing better.

If you dread getting up in the morning to go somewhere, you are going to the wrong place. Trust yourself in the power of endless possibility, because you are the one who holds the key to your own rescue. Attract new ideas, relationships, and opportunities, and learn to become a magnet for every good thing that life has to offer.

Where your focus goes, your energy flows.

If your house is cluttered, so is your mind, so clear out the junk and live your life in a place of power.

Forgive anyone who has caused you pain or harm, and keep in mind that forgiving is not for the benefit of others, it's for you. Just because you forgave does not mean you need to forget, it just means you don't remember anything with anger, which frees up your power and heals your body, mind, and spirit.

As this book says, you will fail your way to success. Everything you have experienced thus far can be used to help you grow as a person, and make your dream happen because you deserve it. If you are sick and tired of being sick and tired, take back your power and create something new in your life. If you were an average person, then you would've had average problems.

Your time on this planet is limited, so don't waste it living someone else's life. Let laughter into your heart, because it's good medicine for your spirit. It makes your immune system stronger and has the power to heal. One minute of laughter can boost your immune system for twenty-four hours, whereas one minute of anger can weaken your immune system for four to five hours.

Do what brings out the best in you, not the stress, because miserable people focus on what they hate about their life whilst happy people focus on what they love. Let go of the things in your life that no longer serve you, and continue to chase your dream.

Read books that inspire and motivate you. Listen to audiotapes on repeat. The best time to listen to motivational tapes is first thing in the morning; this way, they control the spirit of your day.

Look for ways to create multiple streams of income; it's better to have that money and not need it, so work on creating your financial future. Realise who your true friends are that will pick you up when no one else has even noticed you have fallen. I thank Steven and Iftikhar for this every day.

I don't know who you are or what your goals and dreams are, but I do know that they are possible.

I will take this opportunity to thank you for picking up my book; I hope it has made you believe in pursuing your dreams and goals. May God bless you, your dreams, and your goals.

If you ever feel you are alone in your journey, please reach out to me at info @ taharali.com and I will do my very best to assist you in every way possible.

My parting words to you are these: you don't know how your story will end yet, but whatever happens, make sure that nowhere in your text will it ever say that you gave up.

RECOMMENDED READING

My Story from Brick Lane to Dragons' Den by James Caan

In this entertaining book, James Caan, who is a successful entrepreneur and motivational speaker, tells his story at how after dropping out of school at just sixteen, he started his own business. His life in a broom cupboard, without any qualifications and two pieces of fatherly wisdom: 'Observe the masses, do the opposite, and always look for opportunities where both parties benefit'.

Armed with this advice, natural charm and the Yellow Pages, he built a market-leading business with a turnover of £130 million and swiftly became one of Britain's most successful entrepreneurs.

The Real Deal traces both his financial and personal achievements. It offers a frank account of what success at thirty really signifies and brings us right up to the present, including his impact on Dragons' Den and what his charity work, from saving a hospital in London to building a school in Lahore, means to him. Ultimately, it is a story of learning what money is really worth, told by one the country's most insightful businessmen.

RECOMMENDED READING

Maximum Achievement by Brian Tracy

Brian Tracy is one of America's leading authorities on the development of human potential and personal effectiveness.

His exciting talks and seminars on leadership, sales management, and personal effectiveness bring about immediate changes and long-term results.

Brian Tracy is Chairman and CEO of Brian Tracy International, a company specializing in the training and development of individuals and organizations. Brian's goal is to help people achieve their personal and business goals faster and easier than they ever imagined.

He has consulted for more than 1,000 companies and addressed more than 5,000,000 people in 5,000 talks and seminars throughout the US, Canada and 55 other countries worldwide. As a Keynote speaker and seminar leader, he addresses more than 250,000 people each year.

RECOMMENDED READING

Live Your Dreams by Les Brown

As one of the world's most renowned motivational speakers, Les Brown is a dynamic personality and highly sought after resource in business and professional circles for Fortune 500 CEOs, small business owners, non-profit and community leaders from all sectors of society looking to expand opportunity.

As a premier Keynote Speaker and leading authority on achievement for audiences as large as 80,000—Les Brown energizes people to meet the challenges of the world around them. He skillfully weaves his compelling life story into the fabric of our daily lives. The thread is forever strengthened, touting why you can't afford to be complacent and to aim high, achieve and actively make an impact on the world.

He has a keen way of turning what he touches into gold. Over 20 years ago, he won a Chicago-area Emmy for his unsurpassed fundraising pledge drive for the Public Broadcasting System. Followed by several bestselling books and hosting popular national talk shows on television and radio.

Les Brown's straight-from-the-heart, passion and high-energy, motivates audiences to step beyond their limitations and into their greatness in many ways.

RECOMMENDED READING

Secrets of the Millionaire Mind™

NY Times No. 1 Best-seller by T. Harv Eker

Mastering the Inner Game of Wealth. Have you ever wondered why some people seem to achieve wealth effortlessly while others work just as hard but still struggle financially? In this fresh and original book, T. Harv Eker explains how you too can master the inner game of money so that you will not only achieve financial success, but also keep it once you have it.

Using breakthrough techniques T. Harv Eker shows you how childhood and family experiences and inner mental attitudes shape your view of money. Each of us has a personal money and success blueprint already ingrained in our subconscious minds, and it is this blueprint that will determine the course of our financial lives.

Eker reveals: Powerful 'declarations' that drive new, money-attracting beliefs into your subconscious; Dozens of high-income and wealth creation strategies; What truly wealthy people know that others do not; The cause of almost all financial problems; How to earn passive income, so that readers can make money while they sleep.

Armed with insights provided in this book, you can begin taking action to transform your financial self, quickly and permanently.

RECOMMENDED READING

Jane Eyre: Life and Success Coach

Jane Eyre is a successful life and leadership coach with over 25 years of experience in helping people reach their full potential. Working with a variety of clients to develop confidence, resilience, relationships, and effectiveness, she started her career as a teacher before becoming a certified, professional co-active coach. She has a passion for learning and working creatively with people to bring about personal growth, positive change, and impactful results.

Her clients describe her as 'highly effective, powerful and full of perceptive understanding and intuition…empathetic whilst challenging and able to push you beyond what you thought you were capable of. She quickly engages in impactful conversations, asking questions that get you thinking, inviting you to step out of your comfort zone, and enabling you to think about situations in ways you wouldn't do on your own. Moving you forward quickly and helping you stay there.' She is uniquely placed to help you reach your goals.

You can visit her website: www. openeyre.co.uk

ABOUT THE AUTHOR

Tahar comes from humble beginnings to owning a highly successful property investment company conducting over $1billion in sales every year and he's a bestselling author. His passion is helping others live the life of their dreams, be that in business, or personal relationships, or career, and even their health. He has transformed lives with his inspirational talks all over the globe.

He has had successful careers in some of the largest corporations in the world before becoming the successful entrepreneur he is today. His bestselling self-help book, "Fail Your Way to Success" gives an honest account on what it takes to succeed in business and how to create a mindset that can tackle bereavement, depression, anxiety, homelessness, poverty and even business failure.

Tahar is now a prominent speaker and consultant who has challenged and changed the way people think in pursuit of their dreams. He devotes himself to charity work and lives his life with the motto: *'Every day above ground is a good day.'*